ANGELS
of the
BIBLE

FINDING GRACE, BEAUTY, *and* MEANING

KATE MOOREHEAD
with SCOTT BROWN

ISBN: 978-0-88028-473-8
Library of Congress Control Number:2019944306

© 2019 Forward Movement

Forward Movement
inspire disciples. empower evangelists.

ANGELS
of the
BIBLE

FINDING GRACE, BEAUTY, *and* MEANING

KATE MOOREHEAD
with SCOTT BROWN

FORWARD MOVEMENT
Cincinnati, Ohio

Table of Contents

Introduction

Angels stand at the edges of our consciousness. For a variety of reasons, we tend to avoid discussion of them among intellectual circles. But they are there nonetheless, in the greatest of the biblical moments: at the gates of the Garden of Eden, at the birth of Christ, at the tomb of the resurrection. Might it be time to wonder who they are?

Sir Isaac Newton and other enlightenment thinkers drew the conclusion that reality must be based on what can be seen and proven. All else could be considered myth, story, narrative. Protestant theologians in the twenty-first century sought to find a way to take both scripture and Newtonian science seriously. But how could some of these things described in the Bible be true when no one had ever seen them? So we quietly brushed off the miracles of Jesus, the possession of demons, and the appearance of angels. Maybe they happened back then but they don't happen now. As intellectual people, we wondered: Who can take angels seriously while embracing the profound progress of science?

The past few decades have seen the rise of quantum physics—scientific principles that help us understand the wacky and weird behavior of photons, electrons, and other particles that make up the universe. As we have collectively explored quantum physics, we have begun to embrace the idea that not everything has a common-sense answer. Some of the ways of the world are unpredictable and mysterious. This approach to science has led theologians and biblical scholars to wonder once more about the intersection of science and faith. If we perceive reality in only three dimensions but in quantum physics, we accept that there are many more dimensions, could it be possible that angels are flying in front of our faces and yet we cannot see them? What if our perception is limited and miracles and healings and exorcisms and angels are quite possible? What if science has gotten so large and so cosmic that we, in fact, must entertain a reality beyond our visible sight? It seems that we have re-opened the door to miracles and to the awe and wonder of the cosmos.

Though I will occasionally refer to biblical scholarship, this book is primarily devotional. These devotions explore the realm of the mystical, the cosmic, the *mysterium tremendum*. They ponder the *numinous*, as the German theologian Rudolf Otto once described it, the place where God dwells, the realm of the angels.

The devotions include most of the appearances of angels in the Bible (the Old and New Testaments but not the Apocrypha). I have tried to cover all major and significant apparitions to give both a broad and deep exploration of angels in the Bible. If you want to look at every time the word angel appears in either the Hebrew or Greek, I recommend a concordance.[1]

I have designed this book to be used as a daily companion, read in any season, but perhaps particularly poignant during the seasons of Advent and Christmas or Easter, when the apperarances of angels in scripture are numerous. I want us to move into the heart of theological reflection and try to uncover the nuances of these appearances. I believe in order to consider the realm of angels, we must approach these passages from a contemplative state, to meditate on them as one would gaze at a piece of art. Angels cannot be grasped with raw intellect alone. But they can be known relationally as friends, and we can stand in awe of their beauty as we do the stars.

I struggled with how to address angels in regard to pronouns. Many of the angels are described as looking like men in both the Old and New Testaments (Abraham welcomes three men to his table; Mary Magdalene sees a man—or two—in the tomb). Several of the angels are also given male names such as Michael and Gabriel. However, angels are never specifically given gender in scripture, and since they are immortal, it can be assumed that they do not reproduce. It is my assumption that angels somehow transcend gender. With this understanding as the foundation, I use a male pronoun if an angel is described as looking like a man or has a male name. But if the gender is not specified, I will alternate between male and female. The neuter pronoun doesn't work for me simply because angels are so alive and are not inanimate objects.

In order to assist in your contemplation, I have also included depictions of angels through art. We live in a day in which language is shifting. Images are on the rise. The icon of the Starbucks lady speaks louder to us than the words "good coffee." When we see the Starbucks lady, we can taste the coffee. She touches our senses without a word. That is the power of imagery. With each passing year, I increasingly wonder if we are returning to hieroglyphics. From emojis to memes, we are placing images where words once were. Images are faster and more immediately vibrant. They reach us in the blink of an eye and on multiple levels. This is why it seemed futile for me to write a book about angels without including art.

I asked Professor Scott Brown, a friend and colleague, to enrich us with his extensive knowledge of Christian art by selecting paintings to highlight seven pivotal angelic appearances: cherubim at the gates of Eden, Abraham's three guests, Satan testing Job, Isaiah and the seraphim, the annunciation, final battle from Revelation, and the celestial hierarchy. Along with the images, Scott shares the historical and theological context of the paintings. Please take time to meditate on these images. It is my hope that by giving you a taste of the visual, you will become hungry to search for angels in your own lives. I believe that they are there to be found—and can even be seen from time to time.

The Bible asks us to read and digest its stories, not only to recall what God has done before but also to watch for what God is doing now. The Bible is a strange, frustrating, and miraculous text. It contradicts itself and depicts scenes that scare the heck out of me, and yet I truly believe scripture has the capacity to change my life—and yours. If we are to take the Bible as something more than a history book, we must open our minds to the continued existence of angels, and we must look at these apparitions with an eye to understanding our own lives and the role of angels within them.

KATE MOOREHEAD

All Christians are called to ponder the impossible, to look between the worlds at the mystical possibilities that made the incarnation possible. Angels brought the message about Jesus to Mary. Angels sang before the shepherds and appeared to Joseph in dreams. Let us find them amidst the pages of scripture and wonder at their variety and magnificence, for these are the messengers of God.

One

They Should Have Sent a Poet

Thus the heavens and the earth were finished, and all their multitude.

Genesis 2:1

This magnificent verse comes at the end of the first creation story. God has called the world into being in six days and is about to rest on the seventh day. It seems that this new world has been articulated in the six creation proclamations: *Let there be…*light, heavens, dry land and vegetation, stars, aquatic animals and birds, beasts of the earth and humans. But in this beautiful phrase, scripture refers to a mysterious vastness beyond the aforementioned creation, a multitude that is not specified in the language of the ancient writers of Genesis. In other words, there is much more to God's creation than what meets the eye.

Angels are not named as part of God's creation. They simply appear in scripture, sent by God to help humans understand a divine message. Did God create them? Are they uncreated beings, somehow coexisting as part of the very being of God? Since angels are not God, they must be part of the creation, part of the vast array that is mentioned here.

Scripture never tries to explain angels: It simply records their appearances, and these appearances are sporadic and mysterious. Perhaps we are not capable of understanding angels. They seem to be part of a mystical world that transcends our understanding. We are asked only to behold and to listen. Not once in scripture are we asked to understand or rationalize the angelic beings that appear. The Bible never explains who angels are or where they come from; the words of scripture simply direct us to listen to their message, nothing more. For modern American minds, this kind of mystical observation without understanding is frustrating. It is hard to swallow. No wonder we often want to deny the existence of angels. If we can't understand them, it's easier to dismiss them or assume they don't exist at all.

I love the movie *Contact* starring Jodie Foster. A brave young scientist is sent into space using a time/space machine that has been designed by aliens. When Eleanor Arroway, played by Foster, is sent to the outer reaches of the unknown, she sees beauty that she cannot describe with her scientific and mathematical vocabulary. She cries out: "So beautiful! So beautiful! They should have sent a poet." The scientist recognizes her limitations. The phenomena she is experiencing are so vast that they cannot be rationally explained or mathematically calculated; they can only be described with art, poetry, image, and symbol. What she experiences is beyond her comprehension yet touches her senses and moves her heart.

Perhaps angels are best conveyed by poets, painters, and musicians. Perhaps angels will never be fully understood by rational, intellectual minds but only grasped through imagination and the heart. Perhaps, as part of that vast array, angels are meant to be observed but never fully understood or examined. Perhaps they are simply beyond human understanding.

Two

At the Gate of Eden

He drove out the man; and at the east of the Garden of Eden he placed the cherubim, and a sword flaming and turning to guard the way to the tree of life.

Genesis 3:24

After Adam and Eve are expelled from paradise, God places an angel at the threshold between the two worlds. Guarding the gate of Eden, cherubim stand with a burning sword. Cherubim are themselves fiery creatures. In the fifth century, a Syrian monk who would later be referred to as Dionysius the Areopagite wrote a treatise called "On the Celestial Beings." In this treatise, the monk described nine levels of angels, with three kinds of angels in each of three spheres. Cherubim were considered part of the first sphere, the highest of angels, terrifying to behold and full of brightness. Mysteriously, the word cherubim is plural in Hebrew, but the sword that is carried is singular. Is this angel somehow a multiplicity within a single figure? Are there many moving parts within the being? The sword is ever turning as if the cherubim are willing and able to strike out in any direction, reminiscent of the sun itself, which is ever turning and burning. God wants the gate to paradise guarded, and this celestial being is appointed to do the job.

From this moment on, angels will stand on the boundaries between harmony with the Almighty and our fractured human experience. They will guard the paradise to which we no longer belong, but they will not just guard—they will also serve as a doorway, a bridge. They will invite us in, give us announcements, try to open our minds to new realities. They will come to comfort us, yes, but mostly angels will serve as a kind of translator, to bring to us news of cosmic significance, news so large that we would be incapable of digesting it without their help. They will fight for us on the boundaries between the worlds.

The sun rises in the east, where God places the cherubim to guard the gate. All ancient liturgical churches face east, toward the rising of the sun, where new life comes to us each day as a gift. The rising sun will later signify the Son who rises again for us. It is toward the east that we find new life and the presence of paradise that we long for and wish we could see again.

These cherubim are the keepers of the greatest boundary of all creation. They are our guardians but also our protectors from that which we can no longer access or understand. Not this way, the cherubim say. But there will be another way. The rest of scripture chronicles our attempts to return to Eden and our failures in doing so, until Jesus shows us another way.

I recently met three young guards at the security checkpoint of the trauma unit at our city hospital. All three were muscular and physically impressive, one woman and two men. They protected the ill from the crime-ridden streets just outside the doors. When I entered, one man smiled at me in my priestly collar. "I know you are not carrying a gun or a knife, Mother, but I have to check anyway, ok?" Of course I agreed. He looked at me with such kindness, standing there on the divider between the chaos of the street and the order of the hospital. "Thank you for coming to pray with someone tonight," he said.

Cherubim have fiery wings and mysterious, otherworldly qualities. But they too stand on the borders guarding our way to keep us safe and to protect the innocent. I see reflections of them here on earth.

Fig. 3

though Adam and Eve were cast out of paradise, they (and we) were
exiled to a world that is still part of God's creation and still reflects the
logic and rightness of his creation.

In *The Expulsion from the Garden of Eden* (Fig. 3), Renaissance artist
Giovanni di Paolo depicts the angel as before, gently pushing Adam and
Eve toward the exit. God is behind them pointing to a *mappamundi*, a
map of the world and indeed of all creation. God seems to be explaining
to Adam and Eve the nature of the world into which they are entering.
At the center is the earth, surrounded by concentric rings or circles that
symbolize the four elements, the planets, and the zodiac—the whole
of space and time. At this moment of fear and confusion for Adam and
Eve, God is reassuring them that their new home is also part of God's

Art Feature

THE ANGEL OF PARADISE AND THE FIERY SWORD

It is a remarkable fact that our introduction to angels in the Bible involves
one of the darkest and most painful moments in human history. We often
depict angels as beautiful protectors, expressions of God's love, but in
Genesis 3:24, we encounter the first angels in the Bible: cherubim sent by
God to bar Adam and Eve and their descendants from returning to paradise.
In that moment of God's anger and disappointment and of Adam and Eve's
desolation, angels appear to remind us of our guilt and of what we have
lost. The Bible describes these angels, placed before paradise, with "a sword
flaming and turning," to keep watch as guardians of the Tree of Life.

In the religious art of the Middle Ages and the Renaissance, artists often
depicted the cherubim mentioned in scripture as one angel (though there
are many variations), standing between paradise and the forlorn figures of
Adam and Eve, brandishing a sword to remind Adam and Eve that they
cannot return. Representations like these were not usually meant just to
depict the words of the Bible. They were often devotional aids, meant to
inspire reflection on scripture and its meaning. Like any interpretation of
the meaning of a text, such images reflect the way that scripture was read
by the artist and his or her audience. Medieval and Renaissance religious
art thus offers intimate insight into the history of Christian faith.

In a beautiful painting in a medieval copy of the *Bible historiale* (Fig. 1),
for instance, a single angel brandishing the sword gently but firmly raises
his hand to Adam's shoulder and urges him away from paradise, which
is depicted behind the angel as a green place of trees and grass, ringed by
fire. Adam and Eve, slump-shouldered and dressed in tattered animal-skin
clothing, look backward over their shoulders at the angel and raise

their hands in distress, as if speaking. Each of these details gives form to a different idea that gives us insight as to how people in the past read and tried to understand this crucial part of the story of the Fall.

Fig. 1

In this image, the angel depicts a tangible reminder of our sin. He is not cruel or punishing, but his firm touch on Adam's shoulder carries a message. This door to paradise is closed to us, but God has opened a new one: repentance, a door of pardon and forgiveness in Christ, who called himself the door and the gateway to heaven (John 10:9). Interpreters of the Bible have often read the cherubim and the fiery sword as symbols of our return to grace through repentance and faith. The Venerable Bede, an English theologian in the early Middle Ages, suggested that the cherubim represent divine knowledge, sentinels of truth through which we come to know and recognize our own sin. The fiery sword, for Bede, is the "sword of the Spirit, which is the word of God," described by Paul in Ephesians 6:17, by which we must slay our temptations.

Fig. 2

In a famous illustrated psalter from the fourteenth century known [as] the Queen Mary Psalter (Fig. 2), the angel stands in almost exactly [the] same manner, placing his hand on Adam's shoulder. Behind the an[gel,] in the hillock of earth beneath the Tree of Life, the tail of the serpe[nt] who tempted Eve is depicted disappearing into a hole in the groun[d,] reminding the viewer that God punished the serpent too. God curs[ed] the serpent, saying "dust you shall eat all the days of your life," (Ge[n.] 3:14), but God also warned us through the words to Eve that the s[erpent] will lie in wait for her heel. The artist's message is that the serpent, [in a] dark hole in the earth, waits for us still.

First-century historian Philo of Alexandria, who influenced the thi[nking] of the early church fathers, wrote that the cherubim represent God['s] authority and mercy but that the flaming sword flashing about in e[very] direction represents God's reason, in constant rapid motion sparing [what] is good and cutting down what is evil. Versions of Philo's vision of [God] as powerful, merciful, and reasonable have inspired much religio[us]

The Angel of Paradise and the Fiery Sword

It is a remarkable fact that our introduction to angels in the Bible involves one of the darkest and most painful moments in human history. We often depict angels as beautiful protectors, expressions of God's love, but in Genesis 3:24, we encounter the first angels in the Bible: cherubim sent by God to bar Adam and Eve and their descendants from returning to paradise. In that moment of God's anger and disappointment and of Adam and Eve's desolation, angels appear to remind us of our guilt and of what we have lost. The Bible describes these angels, placed before paradise, with "a sword flaming and turning," to keep watch as guardians of the Tree of Life.

In the religious art of the Middle Ages and the Renaissance, artists often depicted the cherubim mentioned in scripture as one angel (though there are many variations), standing between paradise and the forlorn figures of Adam and Eve, brandishing a sword to remind Adam and Eve that they cannot return. Representations like these were not usually meant just to depict the words of the Bible. They were often devotional aids, meant to inspire reflection on scripture and its meaning. Like any interpretation of the meaning of a text, such images reflect the way that scripture was read by the artist and his or her audience. Medieval and Renaissance religious art thus offers intimate insight into the history of Christian faith.

In a beautiful painting in a medieval copy of the *Bible historiale* (Fig. 1), for instance, a single angel brandishing the sword gently but firmly raises his hand to Adam's shoulder and urges him away from paradise, which is depicted behind the angel as a green place of trees and grass, ringed by fire. Adam and Eve, slump-shouldered and dressed in tattered animal-skin clothing, look backward over their shoulders at the angel and raise their hands in distress, as if speaking. Each of these details gives form to a different idea that gives us insight as to how people in the past read and tried to understand this crucial part of the story of the Fall.

Fig. 1

In this image, the angel depicts a tangible reminder of our sin. He is not cruel or punishing, but his firm touch on Adam's shoulder carries a message. This door to paradise is closed to us, but God has opened a new one: repentance, a door of pardon and forgiveness in Christ, who called himself the door and the gateway to heaven (John 10:9). Interpreters of the Bible have often read the cherubim and the fiery sword as symbols of our return to grace through repentance and faith. The Venerable Bede, an English theologian in the early Middle Ages, suggested that the cherubim represent divine knowledge, sentinels of truth through which we come to know and recognize our own sin. The fiery sword, for Bede, is the "sword of the Spirit, which is the word of God," described by Paul in Ephesians 6:17, by which we must slay our temptations.

Fig. 2

In a famous illustrated psalter from the fourteenth century known as the Queen Mary Psalter (Fig. 2), the angel stands in almost exactly the same manner, placing his hand on Adam's shoulder. Behind the angel, in the hillock of earth beneath the Tree of Life, the tail of the serpent who tempted Eve is depicted disappearing into a hole in the ground, reminding the viewer that God punished the serpent too. God cursed the serpent, saying "dust you shall eat all the days of your life," (Genesis 3:14), but God also warned us through the words to Eve that the serpent will lie in wait for her heel. The artist's message is that the serpent, in its dark hole in the earth, waits for us still.

First-century historian Philo of Alexandria, who influenced the thinking of the early church fathers, wrote that the cherubim represent God's authority and mercy but that the flaming sword flashing about in every direction represents God's reason, in constant rapid motion sparing what is good and cutting down what is evil. Versions of Philo's vision of God as powerful, merciful, and reasonable have inspired much religious art.

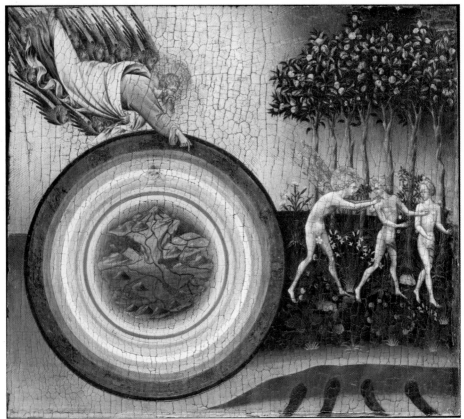

Fig. 3

Though Adam and Eve were cast out of paradise, they (and we) were exiled to a world that is still part of God's creation and still reflects the logic and rightness of his creation.

In *The Expulsion from the Garden of Eden* (Fig. 3), Renaissance artist Giovanni di Paolo depicts the angel as before, gently pushing Adam and Eve toward the exit. God is behind them pointing to a *mappamundi*, a map of the world and indeed of all creation. God seems to be explaining to Adam and Eve the nature of the world into which they are entering. At the center is the earth, surrounded by concentric rings or circles that symbolize the four elements, the planets, and the zodiac—the whole of space and time. At this moment of fear and confusion for Adam and Eve, God is reassuring them that their new home is also part of God's

Fig. 4

plan. Though it will not always be an easy place for them to live, people have their place in this creation, which embodies the rightness of God's reason, though it may sometimes feel as though we are lost in the wilderness, as in another painting of the expulsion by the Renaissance artist Daniel Fröschl (Fig. 4). The guardian angel in the background with his fiery sword may seem frightening but he is a reminder of God's power and grace, urging his creations to renewed faith and to seek a new path to heaven.

Three

SEE ME

The angel of the Lord found [Hagar] by a spring of water in the wilderness, the spring on the way to Shur. So she named the Lord who spoke to her, "You are El-roi"; for she said, "Have I really seen God and remained alive after seeing him?"

Genesis 16:7,13

Hagar is a slave girl. Her body is used by Abram and Sarai to create a child that they could call their own. Her enslavement and rape are the consequence of the old couple's impatience and disobedience: God promised Abram and Sarai a child, but they do not want to wait any longer. And they can't fathom that Sarai's old and barren body could possibly conceive at this point. So the old couple take matters into their own hands and wrong a woman of God.

Not only do they force Hagar to sleep with Abram, but when she does conceive a child, Sarai is consumed with jealousy and banishes her to the desert, away from the safety of their encampment. Hagar is destined to die of dehydration and her unborn child with her. It is at this moment when the angel appears.

The angel ultimately tells Hagar to return to the setting of her enslavement, for there is nowhere else to go. The angel speaks to Hagar as a person—someone of value. And the angel promises Hagar that she will be the mother of multitudes. Her descendants will live for many generations after her, though she cannot conceive of this prophecy at the time. Hagar does not understand all that the angel promises, but she does recognize one important fact: The angel sees her as a person.

Up until this moment, Hagar has not been viewed as human or as worthy of attention. The angel speaks to her despite her status and situation. The angel honors her as a person and as a mother.

To be seen is to exist. We really do not exist until we are seen and known by another. That is why solitary confinement is one of the greatest forms of punishment. We need to be seen by another to see ourselves. We are creatures of community and of relationship.

The angel saw Hagar as a person and spoke to her directly. Hagar believes this angel to be God as she knows no presence more brilliant and more loving.

What does it mean to you to ponder the idea of a celestial being who sees you, watches you, and even delights in you?

Four

MEETING OF THE THREE

So the men turned from there, and went toward Sodom, while Abraham remained standing before the LORD.

Genesis 18:22

The man who is called Abram and his wife Sarai have now been named by God, changed ontologically by their devotion to God, and that change has been given substance in new names: Abraham and Sarah. Three men come and visit Abraham and Sarah at the oak of Mamre. Abraham never asks who they are but treats them as royalty, selecting a tender calf from his herd to slaughter and cook for them. The scripture refers to the three as the Lord. Scholars throughout the centuries have wondered about these three: Were they the Trinity, angels, prophets?

Who they are seems unimportant to Abraham. All that matters to him is that these three come from God. Maybe Abraham understands that he cannot know them fully. He treats them as holy and it is their message that is important, not the specifics of their identity.

Can angels be people? Can the holiness of God reside inside a human being as they speak to another human being? In the scriptures, angels sometimes look or appear as men. A man (or men, depending on the gospel) sit inside the tomb after the resurrection, dressed in white. If any guest could be an angel, then how are we to know who is who? Since it is possible that angels reside in human form, we are called to treat all humans as if they could be messengers of God.

Abraham gives his guests the best that he has. In this way, Abraham ensures his relationship with God remains one of love. How can he know who is who? Can we always tell who is an angel and who is not?

Why not simply receive all guests as if they might be the Holy One and listen to what they have to say? Could it ever be wrong to treat other human beings with the respect and dignity afforded to angels? Abraham trusts in the sanctity of his guests, and they prove him right.

When the three leave, scripture says the Lord remains. Thus the presence of the Holy One seems to move from inside of these three men to a spiritual presence. Abraham continues to speak to the Lord in an uninterrupted flow despite the fact that the three messengers have left him. It is as if he now knows that he does not need an intermediary to talk to God, that God is with him regardless of the presence of angels. The connection is made, and the three figures are no longer needed. In a remarkable dialogue, Abraham begs for the salvation of the cities of Sodom and Gomorrah.

Can angels be the starting point, the introductory relationship of sorts between us and God? Like a matchmaker, they come to us so that we might listen and pay attention to God's message and when we can converse with God without their assistance, they depart. These three seem to have the ability to be present when they are needed and to depart when their mission is accomplished. Having introduced the concept of the pending arrival of Isaac, Abraham and Sarah's birth son, they leave the old couple to argue with God.

Art Feature

ABRAHAM AND THE ANGELS AT MAMRE

Some angelic beings loudly announce themselves in the Bible, appearing to their human witnesses in awesome or dreadful visions, bearing flaming swords, in clouds of smoke, sprouting wings covered in eyes. Others, it seems, appear no different from ordinary men. In the first line of Genesis 18, for instance, we are told that "the Lord appeared to Abraham by the oaks of Mamre, as he sat by the entrance of his tent in the heat of the day." Yet in the very next verse we are told that Abraham "looked up and saw three men standing near him." The reader thus seems to know more than Abraham, a striking instance of dramatic irony. What does Abraham perceive about these "men?" How much does he guess about their natures? This angelic encounter poses questions that invite reflection: How do we recognize God's messengers? Will we know them when we see them?

This dilemma is at the heart of the story of Abraham entertaining his guests at Mamre, a subject that was often depicted in medieval and Renaissance religious art. In these images, as in the Bible, the viewer is usually aware of the angelic nature of Abraham's visitors, while Abraham seemingly is not. The artist often reveals the angels' wings and halos to us, but if we could see through Abraham's eyes, we would see only men. Yet Abraham seemingly behaves as if he knows the men are God's angels. According to the words of the Bible, Abraham bows down before the men and calls them lord. He tells his wife Sarah to prepare fresh bread and commands his servant to slaughter and prepare a calf, and then Abraham himself waits on the men as they eat and refresh themselves.

In art, Abraham is often depicted kneeling, bowing down, even prostrating himself before the men. In one of the most ancient representations of this story, in a mosaic from the sixth century that decorates the cathedral of San Vitale in Ravenna, Italy (Fig. 5), Abraham is dressed as a servant in a short tunic with an apron cloth tied around his waist. He stoops slightly in humility as he carries a platter with the slaughtered calf to the table, where the three men are seated. A small cross adorns the cloth around Abraham's waist, a symbol of this image's meaning. The mosaic is located on a wall of the church just outside the apse, next to the altar. In this setting, Abraham carrying his offering to the Lord's table is an Old Testament model for the offering of the Holy Eucharist on the altar of the church. In fact, the literal meaning of the Latin word *minister* is servant, and Abraham appears in this image as model for the priest or minister as a servant of the church.

Fig. 5

Abraham uses the cloth around his waist to wash his guests' feet, a detail that medieval and Renaissance interpreters often compared to Jesus washing the feet of the disciples. John 13:4 tells us that Jesus tied a cloth around his waist before he began to wash Peter's feet. A beautiful page (Fig. 6) in a medieval German prayer book depicts Abraham washing the angels' feet in a brass basin in an image that closely recalls pictures of

Fig 6

Jesus and the foot-washing from the same time period. In this painting, Abraham is depicted not in a tent, following the words of scripture, but in a large, upper-middle class home of the type common in fifteenth-century Germany. Behind Abraham, the family dogs—a pair of lapdogs—wrestle and play. This image offers us a vision of Abraham as a well-to-do businessman with a nice home in the suburbs and enough money and leisure to keep a pair of purebred dogs as pampered pets. The painting's message is directed at a viewer very much like the person who probably owned this richly decorated prayer book. The message is that prosperous Abraham humbled himself in his own home as a servant to strangers, not because he believed the men to be angels or messengers of the Lord but because this act of humility and service and brotherly love was in his heart. In the image, he is a model for the viewer and the owner of the prayer book, just as Jesus tells his disciples, after washing their feet, "I have set you an example, that you also ought to wash one another's feet" (John 13:15).

In another beautiful image from a late medieval prayer book (Fig. 7), Abraham is dressed as a wealthy gentleman in a fancy hat and wearing rich blue robes embroidered with gold. He presents a platter of food to the angels who are seated at a table dressed with a fine, white, linen tablecloth like the nappe that covers the altar. The angels have no wings but are surrounded by a single, gigantic golden halo, which reflects the artist's interpretation of the three men as the Trinity, three and one. Below the main image, at the bottom of the page, Abraham kneels in prayer before the three men, having removed his hat. Above his head, the artist has depicted a slip of parchment that appears to have been attached to the painted image by golden or brass pins, as though the owner of the book has inserted or clipped a little note to the page. The text on this "note" does not come from Genesis and the story of Abraham but from the Latin Psalms, which were read and spoken as prayers. This passage, from Psalm 50:17 in the Latin Vulgate Bible, is a song of praise for God: *Et os meum annuntiabit laudem tuam* ("And my mouth shall declare thy praise.") The psalm text equates Abraham's humble act of generosity and hospitality with a prayer of praise for the Lord, reminding the viewer perhaps that Jesus himself equated love of God with love of our fellow people: "Just as I have loved you, you also should love one another" (John 13:34). Abraham in these images offers a model for Jesus' commandment and a challenge to the viewer: to treat all who we encounter as though they are messengers of God.

Fig. 7

Five

STAYING THE HAND OF THE SLAYER

Then Abraham reached out his hand and took the knife to kill his son. But the angel of the LORD called out to him from heaven, and said, "Abraham! Abraham!" And he said, "Here I am." He said, "Do not lay a hand on the boy or do anything to him; for now I know that you fear God, since you have not withheld your son, your only son, from me."

Genesis 22:10-12

This is one of the most disturbing stories in all of scripture. After waiting a lifetime for a child, Abraham and Sarah receive their beloved Isaac from God, only to have God demand that Abraham sacrifice the boy as if he were a lamb. Abraham begins to act as the Lord instructs, but at the last moment, an angel saves the day and stays Abraham's hand. An angel stops the violence and rewards Abraham for his obedience.

Yesterday, I stood still and watched as little children were picked up from a school at a bustling intersection. Cars were everywhere. People trying to park, people trying to get past the traffic. Little children, excited to go home, chatted to their parents about their day, wearing crowns (it was Epiphany, and it is a Roman Catholic school). Some children held their parents' hands. Others were too excited, not looking where they were going, talking furiously as children do. Parents seemed frazzled and exhausted. I marveled that no one was hurt.

As I stood there watching, I was overwhelmed by the possibility of angels everywhere. Like crossing guards or traffic controllers, I imagined angels flying from car to car, inspiring care and awareness, conducting the flow of energy so that the scene became a joyful one and not one of tragedy and chaos. Who is to say that they were not there, guiding the hand of the driver or pressing the foot on a brake? Who is to say that the angels were not there as mediators, making this crazy scene flow naturally and gracefully on a Monday afternoon?

We tend to focus on all that goes wrong in our lives—that one time we fell or got sick or were robbed. But so many more times, we avoid accidents by a fraction of a second, looking up and averting danger just before tragedy could strike. To begin to contemplate the action of angels is to discipline our minds to look not only for pain and failure but also to see all that works, all that flows, all that is safe. Let us think of all the days when we live without incident or accident on this fragile and chaotic planet. Is all this harmony and grace chance, or is someone stopping the violence and guiding our bodies and minds? If in fact angels can stop the hand of violence and protect us from each other and even from ourselves, then the ultimate question is this: Why don't they protect everyone all the time? Why are children dying of starvation in Venezuela? Why do bombs tear apart human beings in attacks of terrorism? If angels are powerful, why do they allow this to happen? And ultimately, why did they not stop the crucifixion itself? There is no end to the questions raised from this story of an angel stopping a father from slaying his son.

The Ladder

And [Jacob] dreamed that there was a ladder set up on the earth, the top of it reaching to heaven; and the angels of God were ascending and descending on it. And the LORD stood beside him and said, "I am the LORD, the God of Abraham your father and the God of Isaac; the land on which you lie I will give to you and to your offspring; and your offspring shall be like the dust of the earth, and you shall spread abroad to the west and to the east and to the north and to the south; and all the families of the earth shall be blessed in you and in your offspring. Know that I am with you and will keep you wherever you go, and will bring you back to this land; for I will not leave you until I have done what I have promised you."

Genesis 28:12-15

Jacob is leaving his father and his home for the very first time. He stops for the night and dreams of a ladder or staircase in which angels are ascending and descending from heaven to earth. God stands beside Jacob as he witnesses this mystery and blesses Jacob and his offspring. The Lord promises to remain present with Jacob and to protect him until all these promises are fulfilled.

Angels are going up and down, traveling from earth to heaven and back again. What inspires this movement, this constant back and forthing? Bernard of Clairvaux (1090-1153) spoke of how the angels who love God need to express that love by ministering to those on earth. Bernard wrote that all contemplation of God will lead to action: Angels—and all who approach God in true contemplation—will be filled with such love as to inspire a desire to share that love with others. Thus those who pray, like the angels on Jacob's ladder, are constantly climbing this spiritual path to the divine and then descending to earth to spread the love of God.

Writes Clairvaux, "In this way those blessed spirits…ascend to God's face, they descend to God's pleasure. For he has given his angels charge over you. However, in descending they are not cheated of God's glorious vision, because they always behold the face of the Father."[2]

All prayer leads to this ladder of contemplation and action. We are inspired to pursue God and when we see the beauty of that light and the magnitude of that love, it propels us to return to this broken world to share that love. Love is not to be simply experienced. In its fullness, love is relationship, and the true nature of love is a Trinitarian relationship between God, the devotee, and those who have yet to find God. We are all climbing up and down to God and to others every time we pray. Such is the nature of love. It is not stagnant. It is constant, pure movement, a dance of sorts, like the movement of the planets in their courses. We move to and fro, sharing the love we find in our Maker until the whole earth is full of the knowledge of the love of God.

And the angels show us the way.

Seven

HOLY PLACES

Jacob went on his way and the angels of God met him; and when Jacob saw them he said, "This is God's camp!" So he called that place Mahanaim.

Genesis 32:1-2

Angels of God meet Jacob. And he sees them. Oh, how I wish I could get a description from Jacob about what he saw! So often scripture does not describe angels. And when it does, the descriptions are so brief. Here, Jacob sees multiple angels as he makes his way home after so many years. And he declares the place where he sees the angels as the camp of God.

Is God more potently present in some places more than in others? It seems so. God, the omnipotent and ever-present, is somehow more felt, more experienced in certain locations. And angels are signs of that presence.

Last summer, my husband and I went to Assisi in Italy. I was told to go by my son Jacob, who, at the age of seventeen, told me that he experienced God there.

As soon as we stepped out of the car, I felt something. I cannot describe what it was. Peace, maybe. Profound tranquility. I'm not sure. But something was different. The host took my husband and I to our room at the small inn; without even asking me, my husband said to the host, "Do you have this room available for another night? I think that we may need to stay longer."

Did the lingering presence of Saint Francis cast a spell on us? Was it the prayers of pilgrims for hundreds of years? Or were angels present? Perhaps all three! I certainly believe angels were there in great numbers. The closer we came to Francis's tomb, the holier the space felt. How can you put such things into words?

For the next three days, my husband and I wandered through this small town. I kept returning to Francis's tomb. I felt drawn there. I couldn't help myself. What was this profound presence of peace and beauty? I had no words for it, but it seemed that a host of angels might have been there, just beyond sight, cueing us to the presence of the Almighty. Clearly this particular place had a resonance, a spiritual depth that could only be felt with the heart.

Eight

WRESTLING

Jacob was left alone; and a man wrestled with him until daybreak. When the man saw that he did not prevail against Jacob, he struck him on the hip socket; and Jacob's hip was put out of joint as he wrestled with him. Then he said, "Let me go, for the day is breaking." But Jacob said, "I will not let you go, unless you bless me." So he said to him, "What is your name?" And he said, "Jacob." Then the man said, "You shall no longer be called Jacob, but Israel, for you have striven with God and with humans, and have prevailed." Then Jacob asked him, "Please tell me your name." But he said, "Why is it that you ask my name?" And there he blessed him. So Jacob called the place Peniel, saying, "For I have seen God face to face, and yet my life is preserved." The sun rose upon him as he passed Penuel, limping because of his hip.

Genesis 32:24-31

In one of the most confounding stories in all of scripture, Jacob wrestles with a man. Who is this man? Is he an angel? Is it God? The word Jacob in Hebrew means "one who struggles with God." But surely God is too vast to wrestle a human being? So could this passage be referring to an angel, some kind of messenger or intermediary? Or could it be God made man, like Jesus?

Jacob is alone and cowering in anticipation of the meeting with his brother Esau, whom he wronged many years ago by tricking his father into giving Jacob the treasures of the firstborn (who was actually Esau). Jacob places all of his belongings and livestock and even his wives and children between him and his brother, for fear that Esau will try to kill him. That night, Jacob is confronted with this mysterious man whom he later will call God. Jacob wrestles all night and does not give in. As the dawn approaches, the man wants to leave, and Jacob will not let him go until he blesses him. So the man wounds Jacob by touching his thigh, and he names him Israel, "one who struggles with God."

From this point forward, Jacob's life is joyful (until his favorite son Joseph is sold into slavery. But that's another story!) Jacob's encounter with Esau is full of love and reconciliation. His wealth expands. His children multiply. How fascinating that this strange encounter with God's messenger both wounds and blesses Jacob. He is also renamed through the experience.

We hope our encounters with God will be beautiful, edifying, peaceful. And yet, here is an encounter that is none of those things. It is painful and takes great effort—and the night of wrestling with this man ends up changing Jacob forever.

Jacob's night wrestling with the man gives him a new name to mark the shift. From this point forward, the man declares, Jacob is to be called Israel. (The author of Genesis continues to refer to the man as Jacob and seems to ignore this new name).

Many of us today can probably relate to Jacob's experience as we look back on how times of struggle and pain have changed and transformed us. Don't we learn our best lessons from failure? When I look back on my life, I often grew the most from difficult experiences: the failed test, the bad breakup, the selfish behavior that hurt someone else. Could it be possible that angels were right there with me, helping me to wrestle my ego to the ground and learn a bit of humility or how to alter my behavior? Sometimes love leads to pain as we struggle to remain faithful to one another and as we recognize the times that we have fallen short. Jacob is acting like a coward before he wrestles with this man, and he never behaves like a coward again.

Love often wounds us deeply, yet it is life-altering, humbling, and profound. Jacob realizes this on the night he wrestles and emerges as someone new, renamed, one who will become a great nation.

Nine

ANGEL IN A FLAME

Moses was keeping the flock of his father-in-law Jethro, the priest of Midian; he led his flock beyond the wilderness, and came to Horeb, the mountain of God. There the angel of the LORD appeared to him in a flame of fire out of a bush; he looked, and the bush was blazing, yet it was not consumed. Then Moses said, "I must turn aside and look at this great sight, and see why the bush is not burned up." When the LORD saw that he had turned aside to see, God called to him out of the bush, "Moses, Moses!" And he said, "Here I am."

Exodus 3:1-4

The son of a Hebrew slave, Moses is adopted by Pharaoh's daughter and raised in Pharaoh's house. Moses grows into manhood in the lap of luxury and does not encounter the conflict of his own heritage until he witnesses a Hebrew slave being beaten by an Egyptian soldier. Moses is horrified by the scene and murders the Egyptian soldier. He then runs for his life.

Moses finds a home in the land of Midian, where he marries and tends sheep that belong to his father-in-law. It seems Moses has found a peaceful existence away from the oppressors and the slaves, away from the struggle and violence. But then an angel appears to him in the form of a burning bush, calling him back into the heart of the conflict.

In the Hebrew understanding, it is impossible to see God. Later in Moses' life, he will beg to see the Lord. In Exodus 33, God allows Moses to see what most translations call his back—although the Hebrew for this word more accurately means "where God was." Even when Moses cannot look upon God. The Lord explains that if Moses tries to look at the Almighty, he will die. It is just too much for fragile human beings to gaze upon that kind of power and glory.

So how does the Lord get Moses' attention if Moses cannot see God? The Lord uses an angel to appear to Moses in the form of fire. This fire is unique in that it burns brightly but does not consume the bush. This kind of appearance does not overwhelm or frighten Moses, but it does arouse his curiosity, and he makes the decision to "turn aside and look." Moses exercises free will in this moment. The angel does not frighten him or wave arms up and down, trying to grab Moses' attention. Instead the angel appears in a natural phenomenon that has no rational explanation. Moses is given the choice to notice the miraculous or to pass it by. Thank God Moses chooses to look! Once Moses gives his attention to the fire within the bush, the Lord begins to speak directly to him. The angel never speaks.

I wonder how many times you and I have passed by miraculous things in nature, some thing or moment that could reveal to us God's love or a kind of more specific message from God. I was feeling lonely early one morning as I walked my dogs, and I asked God for a sign of love to reassure me. Suddenly an enormous owl swooped down out of a tree and flew right in front of me, hooting as he went. Could this be a coincidence? Sure. But I chose to see a message within the appearance, and the owl became my messenger, my angel. Moses saw this phenomenon of the burning bush: It caught his attention, yes, but then he made a choice to look further. He took his eyes off of his sheep, his livelihood, his business, and he turned his full attention to God.

So much of the spiritual life is about awareness. It is about turning aside from the busyness of life and looking for a sign of God's love and faithfulness. Moses has sheep to tend. He has lots to do, but he takes his eyes off the practical in order to see the miraculous, and in doing so, he finds his true vocation. He finds himself.

Ten

The Name of God within the Angel

I am going to send an angel in front of you, to guard you on the way and to bring you to the place that I have prepared. Be attentive to him and listen to his voice; do not rebel against him, he will not pardon your transgression since my name is in him.

Exodus 23:20-21[3]

The Lord is in the midst of ratifying the covenant with the Hebrew people. God has liberated them from slavery in Egypt and led them into the desert to the mountain to listen to God's holy ways. And now, God speaks of an angel who will guard them and lead them into the place that is being prepared for them. The angel acts not only as guide but also as instructor. Listen to his words, says the Lord. The angel will not forgive rebellion because "my name is in him."

In Hebrew tradition, the name of a thing possesses a portion of the essence of it. Throughout scripture, we see that when God changes the life of a person, that person is renamed: Abram becomes Abraham, Jacob becomes Israel. So it is a powerful statement to say that God's name is within the angel. The essence of the Almighty is within this being, and this angel is to be heard.

In the Hebrew language, it is impossible to translate the name of God. A clumsy translation is I AM. Yet this is more a statement of simple existence than anything else. God is the only one who has been in existence from before time and beyond. And when we are named, we come into existence as well. When someone speaks our name, it brings us into the present and anchors us in relationship.

Salvador Dali, the famous painter, was born nine and a half months after the death of his brother. His brother's name was also Salvador Dali. The fact that he shared a name with his dead brother confused and wounded Dali deeply. Was he, in fact, his dead brother? Did they somehow share an identity? In his pain and confusion, Dali would later paint a broken picture of his brother.

To be named is to somehow become associated with the essence of the person. And so when the angel is identified as possessing the name of God, it is like saying that there is a portion of divine essence within it. Their identities have merged. The angel has a portion of the divine within it and is therefore worthy to lead the children of Egypt into the Promised Land.

Pay attention, admonishes the Lord, as if the Hebrew people are little children, prone to distraction and forgetfulness. And we are just that, aren't we? We are prone to ignore the guidance of the holy ones, instead rushing about our lives, blindly bumping into one another and causing all kind of problems. The Lord does not tell the Hebrews to talk to the angel or to bring their problems to the angel. Rather, the Lord instructs them (and us) to listen, to pay attention. We are to open our hearts and ears and minds and to follow this angel, whose very being is imbued with the name of God.

Eleven

ANIMALS SEE THEM

God's anger was kindled because [Balaam] was going, and the angel of the LORD took his stand in the road as his adversary. Now he was riding on the donkey, and his two servants were with him. The donkey saw the angel of the LORD standing in the road, with a drawn sword in his hand; so the donkey turned off the road, and went into the field; and Balaam struck the donkey, to turn it back onto the road. Then the angel of the LORD stood in a narrow path between the vineyards, with a wall on either side. When the donkey saw the angel of the LORD, it scraped against the wall, and scraped Balaam's foot against the wall; so he struck it again. Then the angel of the LORD went ahead, and stood in a narrow place, where there was no way to turn either to the right or to the left. When the donkey saw the angel of the LORD, it lay down under Balaam; and Balaam's anger was kindled, and he struck the donkey with his staff. Then the LORD opened the mouth of the donkey, and it said to Balaam, "What have I done to you, that you have struck me these three times?" Balaam said to the donkey, "Because you have made a fool of me! I wish I had a sword in my hand! I would kill you right now!" But the donkey said to Balaam, "Am I not your donkey, which you have ridden all your life to this day? Have I been in the habit of treating you this way?" And he said, "No."

Then the Lord *opened the eyes of Balaam, and he saw the angel of the* Lord *standing in the road, with his drawn sword in his hand; and he bowed down, falling on his face. The angel of the* Lord *said to him, "Why have you struck your donkey these three times? I have come out as an adversary, because your way is perverse before me. The donkey saw me, and turned away from me these three times. If it had not turned away from me, surely just now I would have killed you and let it live." Then Balaam said to the angel of the* Lord, *"I have sinned, for I did not know that you were standing in the road to oppose me. Now therefore, if it is displeasing to you, I will return home." The angel of the* Lord *said to Balaam, "Go with the men; but speak only what I tell you to speak." So Balaam went on with the officials of Balak.*

Numbers 22:22-35

I am the owner of two large Labrador retrievers. The older one, Ella Bella, believes her purpose in life is to make sure squirrels know their place. She doesn't want to catch them; she just wants to make sure they stay in the trees where they belong. Coley, the young 100-pound chocolate lab, cares nothing for squirrels but believes his calling in life is to greet everyone with exuberance and glee, even jumping with joy. Both animals bound out the front door of our house in the early morning with pure joy. If Ella sees a squirrel, she pulls the leash hard. If Coley sees a friend, same. But I am getting older, and I don't like being yanked, so I will sometimes yell and complain in my grumpy morning state. Then, inevitably, I feel guilty. Haven't we all found ourselves impatient and quick to punish an animal for being nothing more than true to itself?

We humans transfer our frustrations and resentments to animals when in reality, animals have not fallen from God's grace. Ella and Coley don't pull on the leash to make me aggravated: they do it for sheer joy. They were never forced to leave Eden. They live in paradise and in the purity of the present moment. They bound forward to meet the day, and I am a bundle of complaints. Animals are truly present in the moment.

In this passage of scripture, the donkey sees the angel when the human being cannot. The donkey protects Balaam by refusing to go where the angel stands guard. His true master is not Balaam; it is the angel. The donkey surely has its priorities straight.

The truth is that animals are a mystery to us. We love them but we will never fully understand them. I do not notice the scents that so captivate my Labrador retrievers. I cannot fathom why my sweet dog insists that all squirrels should be up in the trees and not on the ground, but I can feel her joy when morning comes, and the sun is rising, and we set out to walk together. I do not know what she smells or sees, but I feel her love and the abundance of her enthusiasm.

There is a powerful lesson for us in this story in that it is the donkey who witnesses the angel first. As is all too common among humans, Balaam is consumed with where he thinks he should be going. His sin is in his lack of awareness born of a narrow-minded certainty that he knows the path. The donkey, on the other hand, moves with its eyes wide open.

If we are to see angels, we must first admit that we need to see them, that we are lost and in need of direction. As long as we believe we can do life on our own—that we can find the true purpose of our lives and navigate day by day without guidance or direction—then we will never see the signposts God sets before us, even if they are standing directly in our path.

May our hearts and minds be as open as that of the animals who set off to walk in the early hours of the morning with joy and anticipation, truly awake, and ready to face whatever crosses their path (especially squirrels).

Twelve

An Angel Eats

*Now the angel of the L*ORD *came and sat under the oak at Ophrah, which belonged to Joash the Abiezrite, as his son Gideon was beating out wheat in the wine press, to hide it from the Midianites. The angel of the L*ORD *appeared to him and said to him, "The L*ORD *is with you, you mighty warrior." Gideon answered him, "But sir, if the L*ORD *is with us, why then has all this happened to us? And where are all his wonderful deeds that our ancestors recounted to us, saying, 'Did not the L*ORD *bring us up from Egypt?' But now the L*ORD *has cast us off, and given us into the hand of Midian." Then the L*ORD *turned to him and said, "Go in this might of yours and deliver Israel from the hand of Midian; I hereby commission you." He responded, "But sir, how can I deliver Israel? My clan is the weakest in Manasseh, and I am the least in my family." The L*ORD *said to him, "But I will be with you, and you shall strike down the Midianites, every one of them." Then he said to him, "If now I have found favor with you, then show me a sign that it is you who speak with me. Do not depart from here until I come to you, and bring out my present, and set it before you." And he said, "I will stay until you return."*

So Gideon went into his house and prepared a kid, and unleavened cakes from an ephah of flour; the meat he put in a basket, and the broth he put in a pot, and brought them to him under the oak and presented them. The angel of God said to him, "Take the meat and the unleavened cakes, and put them on this rock, and pour out the broth." And he did so. Then the angel of the Lord reached out the tip of the staff that was in his hand, and touched the meat and the unleavened cakes; and fire sprang up from the rock and consumed the meat and the unleavened cakes; and the angel of the Lord vanished from his sight. Then Gideon perceived that it was an angel of the Lord; and Gideon said, "Help me, Lord God! For I have seen the angel of the Lord face to face." But the Lord said to him, "Peace be to you; do not fear, you shall not die."

Judges 6:11-23

The Israelites are suffering under the rule of the Midianites. They are under so much oppression that Gideon is trying to hide his food by beating out his wheat in a wine press, a process that surely chokes him with dust and chaff in that small space. His people are hungry and desperate. They are convinced God is punishing them.

When the angel appears, his first statement is to encourage Gideon. Not only does he reassure Gideon of God's favor, but the angel edifies Gideon's prowess as a fighter. Gideon's response is a natural one: If I'm so favored, then why is all this bad stuff happening? Where are the miracles? Where is the rescue? The angel responds: You can do it. I commission you. I will be with you.

Gideon is still uncertain about this course of action, so he asks for a sign from God. Then Gideon goes inside his home and prepares his best food to offer to God as a present—in exchange for "a sign that it is" God who is speaking to him. Gideon slaughters a goat in a time when his people are practically starving. While treating a guest with such high offerings is an honored Hebrew tradition, this extravagant hospitality also portends the importance of the sign that is to come.

Gideon places the food on a rock. The angel holds out his staff and touches the food; fire springs up, devouring the food, and the angel disappears. This act convinces Gideon he has entertained an angel. Once more, fire bridges the gap between the heavenly and earthly realms. Just as the cherubim stood at the gate of Eden with fire, so fire demonstrates the presence of the angel with Gideon. And later, in the Book of Acts, the Holy Spirit in the form of fire descends upon the disciples.

What is it about fire that is deemed other worldly? The process of combustion that produces fire changes solid things into dust and smoke. Fire produces heat. It dances and throws off light. To harness fire is to control warmth, prepare food, and sanitize wounds. It is powerful and unpredictable and wonderful. Perhaps it's little wonder that fire is often seen as a sign from heaven.

In this passage, the angel uses fire to consume food. This too is a theme of scripture: At the meal in which we offer food to God, God in turn blesses, feeds, and transforms us. From the table of Abraham to the manna in the desert to the Last Supper, we encounter angels at the table. God wants to feast with us.

Thirteen

THE ONE WHO LEAVES THE PRESENCE OF GOD

One day the heavenly beings came to present themselves before the LORD, *and Satan also came among them. The* LORD *said to Satan, "Where have you come from?" Satan answered the* LORD, *"From going to and fro on the earth, and from walking up and down on it." The* LORD *said to Satan, "Have you considered my servant Job? There is no one like him on the earth, a blameless and upright man who fears God and turns away from evil." Then Satan answered the* LORD, *"Does Job fear God for nothing? Have you not put a fence around him and his house and all that he has, on every side? You have blessed the work of his hands, and his possessions have increased in the land. But stretch out your hand now, and touch all that he has, and he will curse you to your face." The* LORD *said to Satan, "Very well, all that he has is in your power; only do not stretch out your hand against him!" So Satan went out from the presence of the* LORD.*

Job 1:6-12

On a certain day, the heavenly beings present themselves to God. In Hebrew, the phrase literally means the Sons of God. The Sons of God come to present themselves before the Lord. They seem to not dwell perpetually with God in this passage but to be called into God's presence from time to time as one would be summoned by a king or queen. One of the Sons of God is called *The Satan* in Hebrew, which means The

Adversary. Reminiscent of the scene after the fall in Genesis, when God calls out and asks Adam and Eve where they are in the Garden, so God also asks where The Satan has been.

It seems that God has given even the angels free will; as such, Satan has the ability to leave not only the presence of God but also God's awareness. It is strange to hear of God asking where anyone is: Doesn't God already know this? But in order to give us the gift of free will, that comes with love, God must give us the option to leave. Perhaps God can shut off this omniscience, just as I might turn off an app I have on my cell phone that can locate my teenagers' phones anywhere and anytime.

Satan uses his freedom and chooses to leave, to exit the presence of God in such a way that God does not know where he is. To fall from God is to leave God, to exit from God's love and sight. In the Book of Revelation, Satan becomes the poster child of wrong choices. He is the tour guide standing at the exit sign, directing us into the darkness.

The Satan depicted here in the book of Job acts somewhat like a prosecuting attorney (lawyers, please forgive the analogy). Satan's purpose seems to be to contradict God and argue his point as if he were a litigator. When God speaks of Job with pride, Satan dares God to allow him to wreck Job's life as a kind of experiment, to prove that Job's love of God is conditional and will not last if he is confronted with misfortune.

Through Satan's initiative, Job will be forced to travel a path of pain and darkness until all that he loves is taken from him. His loved ones perish, his wealth evaporates, his health deteriorates, and even those friends who sit with him in the dust give him bad advice. The question arises: Will Job follow Satan into total despair, or will he hold on to the light?

Just as the angels protect us and build bridges to God, so it is vital to understand that there is a real presence that is destructive in the spiritual life. Inside of every one of us is the potential destructor, the tempter, the adversary. There can be no true love, no true free will without the option of choosing the alternative. We all have the capacity to hate and to destroy. We all are tempted by the darkness.

When the time comes in our lives and we experience illness, misfortune, or death, we too will sit like Job in the dust and be faced with the choice of all choices. Do we rejoice even in the midst of pain and suffering as Jesus did? Or do we blame and learn to hate? The choice is ours just as it was Job's. We are human beings, created in the image of God and free to choose to love or to leave the presence of the Almighty. We are free to draw closer or to move farther away into the darkness.

Job's story raises the question many have pondered: Why does God allow us to suffer? I intend to ask this question in the hereafter but until that time, I don't think I am capable of understanding the answer. What I can do, however, is remember the real influence of dark angels, the demons, the adversaries. They exist, and they can influence us, but even our awareness of their process can diminish their influence. Shine light on them, and they dissolve in its brightness.

Art Feature

JOB, SATAN, AND SUFFERING IN THE DIVINE PLAN

The Book of Job is one of the great works of world literature, of moral philosophy, and of cosmology. It is a story that, through the suffering of one man, helps us to imagine the infinite complexity of the logic of God's universe, including the roles of the angelic being Satan in the divine plan. The story of Job turns on deeply human experiences of loving, suffering, yearning, despairing, blaming, and enduring. There is great material for religious art and spiritual contemplation in this deeply philosophical book, but there are few "famous" images of Job in the history of art. Many if not most artistic representations of Job are deeply personal objects made for private individuals and, often, for people of modest means. Historically, artists have made images of Job not for kings and queens desiring high art but for ordinary men and women seeking insight into human suffering and faithful endurance. This is a reminder that Job speaks to all of us, the rich and the poor, the high and the low, but perhaps we hear him better when we, too, in disgrace and outcast state are tempted to curse fate.

Images of Job in medieval and Renaissance art often give us a means of intimate connection across the centuries to our forbearers. A seventeenth-century pottery plate (Fig. 8), for instance, an example of Delftware, depicts Job in misery on the dung heap, according to the words of Job 2:8. At this point, Job has already suffered at Satan's hands the loss of his wealth, his home, his children, and his health. He sits on the dung heap scraping his boils with a potsherd, a fragment of pottery like that of the plate itself, which perhaps partly explains the choice of subject for the plate's decoration. The image of Job in this context has deep poetic and spiritual meaning: The plate is the practical symbol of providence and the tangible reminder of our duty of thanksgiving. We are reminded by Job that others suffer in privation even as we sit to eat in prosperity.

Fig. 8

In the Bible, Job's wife and former friends visit him when he is at his
lowest point, not to console him but to try to explain for themselves
how Job's misfortunes came to pass. These scenes of Job on the dung
heap visited by his wife and his peers are the most common artistic
subjects in the representation of the Book of Job. Like the Delftware
plate, many of these images are small, humble, personal objects. During
the Renaissance and the era of the Reformation, simple prints on paper
were quite common. They could be produced and sold cheaply and were
collected by ordinary people as devotional and contemplative models.
An image by the German protestant artist George Pencz is typical (Fig. 9).
The artist condenses several parts of the story into one scene: Job is
seated on a rubbish heap. His wife bears the body of one of his children;

a servant standing next to Job gestures to emphasize this tragic loss; a gentleman in a large hat, probably Job's friend Eliphaz approaches from the right; and a servant waving his arms runs in front of Job's burning house. On the far left, unseen by any of the people in the image, Satan appears as a monstrous creature stretching forth a claw as if to take Job in his clutches.

Fig. 9

In the story alluded to by the artist, Job's wife urges him to blame God, to curse God and die. Job's friends, led by Eliphaz, insist that Job himself must be to blame, arguing that suffering is punishment of sin and that only the wicked suffer. When inexplicable tragedies happen, we often want to find something to blame. Job's story points out a difficult truth: Casting blame may feel good, like we are solving a problem, but blaming is not the same as explaining or understanding. Job rejects his friends' transactional concept of grace and providence and their conclusion that if you are rich then you must be righteous, if miserable then you must have sinned. He seeks a deeper understanding.

Images of Job operate like metaphors that point toward a more profound explanation. In an orderly and logical universe, Job's dung heap is the artist's symbol of disorder. It is a formless, shapeless, earthy mass, as far in form from a perfect universe as we can imagine. In a typical painting in a medieval prayer book (Fig. 10), for example, the dung heap disrupts the orderly geometric background of the image like a stain on a beautifully woven fabric.

Fig. 10

In art, it is usually at the dung heap that we see images of Satan afflicting Job. Satan, like the dung heap, is also disordered in religious art. He is usually depicted as a monstrous being of mismatched parts: a deformed and distorted mass of beaks, claws, tails, and mouths. These signs of disorder are metaphors of Job's alienation from God. In suffering and tragedy, we feel often that something has gone wrong with God's plan. Even Jesus demands, before his death on the cross, "My God, my God, why have you forsaken me?"

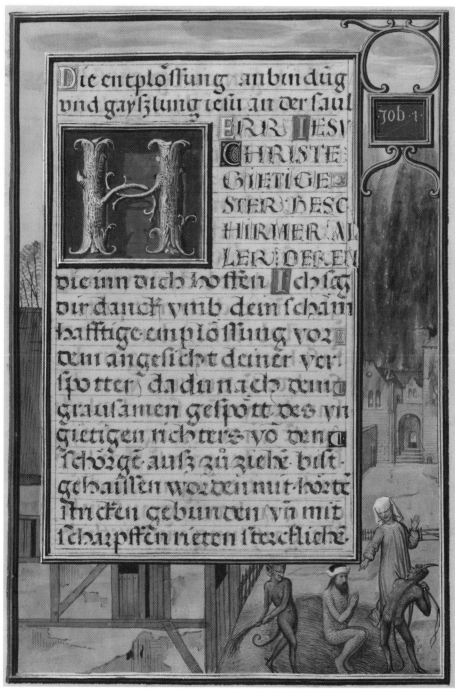

Fig. 11

How can such suffering be part of the divine plan? In some medieval interpretations, Job's affliction on the dung heap is compared to the flagellation of Christ, a trial of the spirit and the flesh, as in an image from a late medieval German prayer book (Fig. 11), in which devils play the roles of the men who scourged Christ.

Fig. 12

Other artworks depict Job's more philosophical search for answers for suffering. An exquisite medieval Book of Hours, a type of prayer book, depicts Job staring at God in heaven while gesturing to a flower (Fig. 12). The words below the image are quoted from Job 14:1-2, Job's prayer to God: *Homo natus de muliere, brevi vivens tempore, repletur multis miseriis...* "A mortal, born of woman, few of days and full of trouble, comes up like a flower and withers, flees like a shadow and does not last."

When God answers Job's complaint near the end of the book, he answers from a whirlwind, a figural metaphor that is the opposite of the dung heap. Where the dung heap is inert, the whirlwind is active. Where the dung heap is a disordered mess, the whirlwind is a chaos of forces whose order is beyond the limits of our natural perception and comprehension. An engraving by the Dutch artist Adriaen Collaert (Fig. 13) attempts to give form to God's answer to Job: His extraordinary image depicts a heavenly host of seraphs and cherubs and angels playing divine music and whirling in complex concentric circles around the Tetragrammaton, the mystical name of God, above the globe of the earth. The artist imagines a divine Physics, a metaphysical vision with the mathematical order of Isaac Newton's calculus, assuring the viewer that even Job's dung heap—and our private miseries—are inscribed within the infinite order of God's moral and physical universe.

Fig. 13

Fourteen

GUARDIAN ANGELS

For he shall give his angels charge over you, *
to keep you in all your ways.
They shall bear you in their hands, *
lest you dash your foot against a stone.

Psalm 91:11-12

The psalmist speaks of angels guarding us, protecting us from falling.[4] This notion is very primal, the notion of some kind of cosmic protector that will save us from evil. Every child wants a guardian angel to slay the monsters and the bad guys. We feel inherently vulnerable in the dark, when we experience unexpected tragedy, or when we ponder the fragility of this planet, floating in the universe with nothing to protect it from meteors or other cosmic events.

Could it be that God arranges some kind of heavenly assistance to keep us from simply destroying ourselves? Given the human propensity for destruction and chaos, I think this is likely. Could God (and God's angels) be playing an unseen role in our nuclear-weapon standoff, protecting us without our knowledge from arming and firing these weapons of mass destruction?

The truth is that even our physical world balances on a thread. We humans live on a very small portion of the planet, where the pressure is just so, the air just right. We cannot survive if we fly too high into the sky or dig too deep into the earth, not without technological assistance to breathe. And yet we have survived for millions of years.

Balance takes effort. When I stand on one foot, my standing leg is working back and forth, with minute adjustments, to maintain the physical existence is just as precarious, might there be divine forces working to keep us upright? Do we, in fact, have angelic protectors?

To conceive of a guardian angel of any kind is to remember what it felt like to be held as a tiny child, to relax into the arms of someone much larger and wiser, someone who knows you and accepts your vulnerabilities, someone who loves you wholly and unconditionally. Only a protector from God could comfort us in such a way. Only an angelic embrace could make us feel truly safe. This is what the psalmist promises: There are angels out there, and they are holding you up.

Fifteen

Seraphim

In the year that King Uzziah died, I saw the Lord sitting on a throne, high and lofty; and the hem of his robe filled the temple. Seraphs were in attendance above him; each had six wings: with two they covered their faces, and with two they covered their feet, and with two they flew. And one called to another and said: "Holy, holy, holy is the LORD of hosts; the whole earth is full of his glory."

Isaiah 6:1-3

Dionysius the Areopagite, the Athenian that Paul converted to Christ as recorded in the Book of Acts, was one of the first theologians to try to make order out of the realm of angels. In *The Celestial Hierarchy*, he describes nine levels of angels bridging the gap between humanity and the divine, three levels of three beings, like three separate dimensions of divine encounter. At the bottom of this hierarchy are angels who interact directly with humans; next are archangels. At the highest level of all are the seraphim.

The word *seraph* means fire-maker, carrier of warmth in Hebrew. The *seraphim* literally burn with love of God, and they hover above the divine throne in a kind of blazing ecstasy. Like the rays of the sun, they illumine the presence of God. Their six wings make them seem entirely otherworldly and, of course, they don't speak. Instead they sing, eternally chanting what we now sing at the altar in the Holy Eucharist, the *sanctus*, using the word holy to praise God and sing of glory.

Scripture mentions the word seraph only once: here in this passage from Isaiah. The prophet witnesses the seraphim, this highest of states, in a vision and when he throws himself down and declares himself unworthy to be in this holiest of places, a seraph comes to him with a burning coal and puts it on his tongue. From that moment, his sins are burned away, and he is called into prophecy. Transformed by the burning presence of the seraphim, Isaiah becomes an agent of God's will.

Something about that burning coal alters Isaiah. It is as if a bit of the blazing ecstasy of the celestial being is placed into his body, perhaps transforming him in a way similar to our experience when we take the host into our mouths during eucharist. This encounter of Isaiah and the seraphim is primal, the feeding of a human being, placing something in his mouth as if he were an infant. And yet, at the same time, the encounter is completely transcendent and otherworldly.

Many know and love the story of Saint Francis, who lived at the turn of the twelfth century. Francis gave up his wealthy heritage to wander the Italian countryside near Assisi, to embrace and love fully all the creatures of the earth, and to praise God for his handiwork.

What is lesser known about Francis is that he too had a vision of a seraph. It happened at the end of his life. He went alone to pray for days on end and had a vision of a seraph that appeared in the form of Jesus on the cross and yet was burning and had wings. The seraph touched Francis during the vision, and the encounter produced a constant bleeding in Francis's hands, feet, and side, just as if he bore the wounds of Christ himself. This was first time that the stigmata had occurred in human history.

This pain, this burning that Isaiah describes, seems to be part of the encounter with the seraphim, the highest form of celestial being. Perhaps the closest comparison we have is to burning coals and fire.

When the risen Christ appears to the disciples on the road to Emmaus, they are invigorated and discuss scripture with him, not knowing it is their Lord. After they invite him home and he blesses their food, their eyes open and they recognize Jesus. They are so startled and moved by the encounter that they decide to walk back to Jerusalem to tell their friends. While they are walking back, they try to describe what it felt like to talk with the risen Christ. Searching for words, they use images of their hearts burning. They ask: "Did not our hearts burn within us while he was on the road with us?" God loves us so, and we love God such that our hearts burn and rise to him. And when we get to the throne, if we ever can get that close to love itself, we shall see the seraphs burning fire.

Isaiah and the Seraphim

One of the most interesting things about the Bible's angels is that they are so different from each other, at least in the ways that people see, feel, or otherwise perceive angelic beings. Adam and Eve are confronted by a flaming sword, Abraham sees men, and Job knows nothing of Satan but suffers his presence. Others, especially prophets, are treated to the most extraordinary, supernatural visions—fiery, smoking scenes of terrifying six-winged creatures or four-handed, four-faced "living creatures" like unto men, eagles, lions, bears, calves, and leopards. Some are covered along the length of their bodies in eyes; they speak or sing a heavenly but overwhelming music in voices of thunder and lightning that rattle the thresholds. These beings are awesome and powerful, bearing in their midst a throne with the Lord of Hosts, God Almighty, seated in dreadful majesty. The witnesses to these extraordinary visions are generally overwhelmed, quite understandably. Isaiah despairs, "Woe is me! I am lost." Ezekiel falls flat on his face. John, in the Book of Revelation, is overcome by emotion after fainting away as though dead.

These angels, seraphs, cherubs, and the living creatures are the most fantastical and perhaps unbelievable sights in scripture. The prophets themselves hardly believe their eyes or know what to make of their visions. But this is not surprising. Scholars who study vision—philosophers, psychologists, scientists, art historians—have long been aware that human vision is a complex and faulty faculty of understanding. There are physical differences and limitations on human sight (nearsightedness, farsightedness, color blindness, etc.) and perceptual challenges (we notice and attribute significance to different things), and of course, limits of perspective. We cannot see or perceive

Fig. 14

the very small or the very large. At both extremes our scientists and
theologians are chasing shadows and theorizing what lies beyond the
boundaries of vision: the particles of the soul, the infinite horizon of
the universe.

In the Middle Ages, theologians believed that there were four kinds of
sight. Corporeal vision is the normal kind, rooted in our bodies, but
symbolic vision, the second level, was a form of deeper understanding.
When Job points at the fading flower and sees a symbol of the
temporariness of life, he grasps a truth about God's creation. To "see with
the eyes of the heart" was a third kind of sight in medieval spirituality.
This perhaps is how Abraham perceives his angelic visitors, who
outwardly appear to be men. The eyes of the heart take us closer to the
spiritual truth of things. The final kind of vision is the rarest and most
special: anagogical vision, the direct elevation of the senses into heaven,
a direct contact with God. When John sees the four living creatures,
he literally sees through a door in heaven, as depicted for instance in
an illustrated medieval copy of the book of Revelation (Fig. 14). John
stands outside the framed painting, looking through a small door in the
picture frame at the heavenly host of angels and elders singing a divine
song of praise for God enthroned in their midst.

Fig. 15

This song, which begins "Holy, holy, holy, Lord God Almighty," reprises
the song sung by the seraphs in Isaiah's vision hundreds of years before
John: This is the *Sanctus*, the hymn sung in our liturgy before the rite of
Holy Eucharist. "Holy, holy, holy is the Lord of hosts; the whole earth is
full of his glory," sing the seraphs in Isaiah's vision in voices that shake the
temple, which fills with heavenly smoke from their presence. In the liturgy,
especially of the Middle Ages, priests swinging censers fill the church
with clouds of fragrant incense in memory of Isaiah's vision. A beautiful,
golden, medieval reliquary chest with vibrant enamel decorations (Fig. 15)
depicts angels swinging censers on either side of the hand of God above an
image of Christ apocalyptic, with the letters Alpha and Omega inscribed
on either side of his halo. On the opposite side of the chest (Fig. 16), the
four living creatures of John's vision appear in graceful abstraction to the
left and right of exquisite interlace medallions, figural metaphors for the
complexity and elegance of the design of God's universe. The chest would
have stood on the altar, bathed in the odor of the sanctifying incense, the
voices of the choir and the tones of the *Sanctus* reverberating around it, a
vision of Isaiah's temple in resplendent miniature.

Fig. 16

Isaiah's clouds of smoke and those of the smoking censers, which
obscure the action of the corporeal eyes, may actually allow us to see
farther or truer with the eyes of our hearts, sharpening our inner senses
by dulling the organs of sight. Likewise, the seraphs' music is like
a cloud of sound that overwhelms the ear with its majestic and all-
pervading thunders. We hear something like it in the full-throated roar
of the church organ, all stops open, shaking the rafters of the church but
lifting our hearts toward God. In medieval and Renaissance art, images
of seraphs often express this idea symbolically. The visions of seraphs
imagined for us by human artists urge the viewer to see beyond the
limits of physical sight, to look past the paints, colors, lines, and shapes
that make the picture and to perceive a little more clearly the glorious
truth toward which the pictures gesture.

An exquisite Renaissance prayer book, for instance, depicts Christ as
Salvator Mundi, savior of the world, in a golden aura ringed by red
seraphs (Fig. 17). A painted scroll below Christ bears the prayer, *Salve
sancta facies* ("Hail, O holy face of our redeemer"). The seraphs are a

Fig. 17

Fig. 18

reminder from the artist to us that we are not to dwell on the material image but to look deeper, to seek true sight like Isaiah's of our Lord Himself. A painting by the Renaissance master Andrea Mantegna (Fig. 18) of the Virgin and Child surrounded by seraphs and cherubs also urges the viewer to look past the designs made by the imperfect hand of the artist, to see the true meaning of Christ incarnate, who became human for us. This also is the idea conveyed by an elaborate, illuminated initial (Fig. 19) in a late medieval gradual, a hymnbook.

In the hymnbook, the letter "A" frames an image of Christ enthroned in the midst of angels and saints. Below, outside the frame, the tail of the left edge of the initial curls around a tiny image of Isaiah, who gazes raptly up at the heavenly sight. The initial is the first letter of the hymn, *Aspiciens a longe ecce*: "Watching from afar, behold, I see the power of God coming." This song, based on Isaiah's vision, was sung in the medieval liturgy at the beginning of Advent. Its words, thrilling in the voices of the choir, urge us also to behold from afar, to look for that truth which our eyes alone cannot show us.

Fig. 19

Sixteen

The Thrones

In the thirtieth year, in the fourth month, on the fifth day of the month, as I was among the exiles by the river Chebar, the heavens were opened, and I saw visions of God. …

As for the appearance of their faces: the four had the face of a human being, the face of a lion on the right side, the face of an ox on the left side, and the face of an eagle; such were their faces. Their wings were spread out above; each creature had two wings, each of which touched the wing of another, while two covered their bodies... As I looked at the living creatures, I saw a wheel on the earth beside the living creatures, one for each of the four of them. As for the appearance of the wheels and their construction: their appearance was like the gleaming of beryl; and the four had the same form, their construction being something like a wheel within a wheel. When they moved, they moved in any of the four directions without veering as they moved. Their rims were tall and awesome, for the rims of all four were full of eyes all around. When the living creatures moved, the wheels moved beside them; and when the living creatures rose from the earth, the wheels rose. Wherever the spirit would go, they went, and the wheels rose along with them; for the spirit of the living creatures was in the wheels. When they moved, the others moved; when they stopped, the others stopped; and when they rose from the earth, the wheels rose along with them; for the spirit of the living creatures was in the wheels.

Over the heads of the living creatures there was something like a dome, shining like crystal, spread out above their heads. Under the dome their wings were stretched out straight, one toward another; and each of the creatures had two wings covering its body. When they moved, I heard the sound of their wings like the sound of mighty waters, like the thunder of the Almighty, a sound of tumult like the sound of an army; when they stopped, they let down their wings. And there came a voice from above the dome over their heads; when they stopped, they let down their wings.

When I saw it, I fell on my face.
Ezekiel 1:1,10-11, 15-21, 22-26

How do we make sense of the many titles and words used to identify different kinds of angels? Dionysius the Areopagite tried to make sense of the angels by creating a kind of map to sort them out and determine their places in the heavenly realm. He painted a picture of three levels of celestial beings, with each level containing three specific types of angels. At the highest level, closest to the throne of God, are the seraphim, cherubim, and the thrones.

Dionysius drew from the Greek word *thronos* used by Paul in Colossians 1:16. These throne angels are considered the same as the wheels described in Daniel and Ezekiel. They relate closely to the cherubim, which Ezekiel describes as having four faces and which will later become symbolic of the writers of the four gospels. Ezekiel explains that these wheels or thrones move when the cherubim move, almost as if they are united by one energy and one spirit. These spheres rotate in circles and are covered with eyes, ever watching and observing. The brightness of these spherical beings is so overwhelming to Ezekiel that he falls on his face.

How do we explain such alien phenomena? It is one thing to contemplate angels that basically look like people, even if they radiate light and have multiple wings. But Ezekiel's vision of thrones is more cosmic in nature, other-worldly even. When we as humans try to imagine creatures beyond our world, we usually devise some wacky variations on things we already have seen: giant bugs, over-sized dinosaurs, vicious reptiles, all with extra eyes, legs, teeth, wings, etc. But Ezekiel sees creatures that don't look like anything he knows; his closest comparison is a wheel that seems to rotate and radiate light and awareness at the same time.

Something about Ezekiel enables him to see with spiritual eyes, to perceive of things that most of us cannot. What makes him capable of taking in such cosmic phenomena? What makes him able to see? Biblical scholar David Creech notes that in some ways, Ezekiel's visions and writings are the product of his own creativity and the images are often symbolic. Ezekiel points to our capability for creativity in discerning and describing the divine.

The more I pray, the more I realize that we are blind, that we block out the movement of angels and the workings of God. We can only take in so much information, and so we choose to see what physically lies in front of us. We hesitate to close our eyes and open our imaginations to something more. We are afraid, and so we protect ourselves by contemplating our physical existence alone and revisiting the same thoughts and worries over and over again.

Jacques Lusseyran was blinded at the age of eight in 1932 when he fell and hit his right eye on the corner of a table at school. Although he was wearing shatterproof glasses, the arm of the glasses pierced the tissue of his right eye. The blow was so powerful that it caused what is now called sympathetic ophthalmia, and the retina of his left eye was torn as well. Both of his eyes had to be removed.

The result of this injury was that Jacques began to learn to see in new ways. His extraordinary parents did not try to protect him out of fear but encouraged his contemplation and exploration. He began to "see" the morality of a person by the tone of that person's voice. He began to feel that stagnant objects were actually moving. (This was way before science would agree with him). But in order to "see," Jacques learned that he had to be free of anger, fear, and self-pity. These feelings clouded his observations. They literally blinded him.

Jacques ended up becoming a hero of the French Resistance in World War II. He was able to discern who was speaking the truth and who was planting lies and misdirection as a spy. Jacques was eventually sent to a concentration camp where he learned to see beyond the pain, and ultimately, he survived.

Rather than asking ourselves if Ezekiel really saw the vision as he reported it, what if we asked ourselves how we could see like he did? Can you become more aware of your dreams? Do you sit still and contemplate the heavens? Do you shut your eyes and listen to the movement of the world around you? Everything is indeed spinning, isn't it?

Seventeen

Protector in the Lion's Den

When he came near the den where Daniel was, he cried out anxiously to Daniel, "O Daniel, servant of the living God, has your God whom you faithfully serve been able to deliver you from the lions?" Daniel then said to the king, "O king, live forever! My God sent his angel and shut the lions' mouths."

Daniel 6:20-22a

Daniel is a devout Jew living in Babylon. As a bright and accomplished man, Daniel quickly rises to the top of the government, reporting directly to the king. Jealous courtiers trick the king into issuing a decree against the Jews, and the king is forced to send Daniel to the lions' den, where he is sure to be devoured. Daniel prays fervently and enters the den. The next morning, the king rushes to the den and calls for Daniel. Daniel is unharmed! He answers the king, assuring him that God sent an angel to shut the mouths of the lions. Daniel emerges from the lions' den without a scratch.

We often talk of evangelism, of sharing the gospel with others, but words without action can be easily dismissed, and hearts are left unmoved. What brings people to God time after time is when they witness a person of faith who is suffering but does not despair. When people see that death, pain, and misfortune cannot overcome our belief in a benevolent creator, then we become evangelists like Daniel.

In the ancient text *The Passion of St. Perpetua, St. Felicitas and Their Companions*, we hear the story of a twenty-two-year-old woman who is executed for her belief in Christ at the beginning of the third century. No angels intervene to stop the executioners, but Perpetua seems at peace. Throughout the centuries of Christian martyrdom are many stories of believers going to their deaths while praising God, their spirits untouched even as their bodies are mangled. This kind of living sacrifice, made joyfully, has been a mark of Christianity from the earliest days.

All over the world, religious people suffer for their belief. Houses of worship are bombed, worshipers shot, fires started. Muslim, Jewish, Christian. No matter the tradition, people have been killed simply for practicing their faith. Why doesn't God send an angel to disable the bomb, reason with the arsonist, or convince the shooter to lay down the weapon? Where have the angels been? Why does God save the lives of some but not others?

I have no answer for these hard questions. All I can see is the image of Daniel, brave and true, who goes into the lions' den because of his belief. I wonder if angels always come when we make sacrifices for our faith. Maybe they will greet us on the other side.

Eighteen

GABRIEL, PRINCIPALITIES, AND POWERS

While I was speaking, and was praying and confessing my sin and the sin of my people Israel, and presenting my supplication before the LORD my God on behalf of the holy mountain of my God—while I was speaking in prayer, the man Gabriel, whom I had seen before in a vision, came to me in swift flight at the time of the evening sacrifice. He came and said to me, "Daniel, I have now come out to give you wisdom and understanding."

Daniel 9:20-22

Daniel is old. He has lived a long life in the court of many kings and been able to remain true to his faith while also earning the trust of the monarchs. In this passage, Daniel is mourning the sins of his people and the state of his beloved city Jerusalem. While fasting and praying, Daniel encounters the angel Gabriel as well as a vision of an unnamed man. In all his visions, Daniel is told that archangels and other forms of celestial beings are involved in politics and in the warring of nations. Not only are there the physical realities of the present struggles on earth, but there is a battle of some kind going on in a spiritual realm and the two are interrelated.

This theme of a cosmic battle will be carried into the New Testament, especially in the Book of Revelation. It is as if the struggles we engage here on earth are mere reflections of a greater war going on in the heavenly world, an ultimate battle between light and darkness, good and evil. And the warriors on both sides are angels.[6]

Sometimes this physical manifestation of spiritual warfare is palpable. Visitors to Nazi Germany in the 1930s describe a sense of menace that seemed to hang in the air. Journalists covering apartheid South Africa have described feeling a weight of injustice on their shoulders. When I visited Jerusalem, I felt a foreboding sense of conflict, of a war between the forces of darkness and the light.

Institutions, governments, and societies have a kind of spiritual presence. Some call it "vibe," others call it culture, but this presence is real. Walter Wink, in his book *Engaging the Powers*, writes, "Any attempt to transform a social system without addressing both its spirituality and its outer forms is doomed to failure. Only by confronting the spirituality of an institution *and* its concretions can the total entity be transformed, and that requires a kind of spiritual discernment and praxis that the materialistic ethos in which we live knows nothing about."[7]

What might happen if we began to pay attention to this spiritual intuition? What if we engaged in the kind of listening and observation that could lead us to challenge systems that seem corrupt at a deep level? We can only wonder how this type of approach could have changed the course of history.

But we still have an opportunity today to hone and listen to our spiritual intuition. The United States is divided and polarized to an extent that I cannot recall in my lifetime. Americans argue the issues with passion but few step back to ponder why our culture and media insist on black-and-white answers to complex issues. How can immigration or unemployment or crime be reduced to sound bites? The notion that one side is right and the other wrong comes from a place of dangerous simplicity. Our basest, lowest-level nature assumes we have the answers to the world's complex problems and that if people would just come to our side, agree with our positions, the issues would be solved. This desire for easy fixes, assumed simplicity, and raging passion without thorough education deepens our divisions and cripples our country and its freedoms.

Who are we at war with? Is it one another? Don't all Americans want to live in peace and relative comfort? Are compromises not possible? Perhaps a first step toward peace is to sit back in contemplation and ask ourselves some critical questions: What is the real adversary in our current system? How can we bring this adversary into the light? How can we engage the angels of light to help us come to an understanding that involves true communication, mutual respect, and honest discourse?

Daniel hears the angel speak of an anointed one who will come and save the earth from destruction. When Jesus comes, many look to these apocalyptic visions of Daniel and see signs of the coming of Christ. Is this what the angels mean? Will God send us a Savior? Let us move into the New Testament and see how the angels announce the arrival of Christ.

Nineteen

ANGELS AT BIRTH

Once when [Zechariah] was serving as priest before God and his section was on duty, he was chosen by lot, according to the custom of the priesthood, to enter the sanctuary of the Lord and offer incense. Now at the time of the incense offering, the whole assembly of the people was praying outside. Then there appeared to him an angel of the Lord, standing at the right side of the altar of incense. When Zechariah saw him, he was terrified; and fear overwhelmed him. But the angel said to him, "Do not be afraid, Zechariah, for your prayer has been heard. Your wife Elizabeth will bear you a son, and you will name him John. You will have joy and gladness, and many will rejoice at his birth, for he will be great in the sight of the Lord. He must never drink wine or strong drink; even before his birth he will be filled with the Holy Spirit. He will turn many of the people of Israel to the Lord their God. With the spirit and power of Elijah he will go before him, to turn the hearts of parents to their children, and the disobedient to the wisdom of the righteous, to make ready a people prepared for the Lord." Zechariah said to the angel, "How will I know that this is so? For I am an old man, and my wife is getting on in years." The angel replied, "I am Gabriel. I stand in the presence of God, and I have been sent to speak to you and to bring you this good news. But now, because you did not believe my words, which will be fulfilled in their time, you will become mute, unable to speak, until the day these things occur."

Luke 1:8-20

An angel appears in the temple. Imagine that! I believe our houses of worship are filled with angels that we have invited in with our praise. The angel was probably at the altar all along, but in this particular moment, Zechariah's eyes are open to see him.

In the gospels, angels often tell those who see them to be not afraid. If their first words are words of reassurance, then we can assume that their physical appearance must be frightening. Zechariah is probably shocked. The angel Gabriel comes to give Zechariah news that he will have a son. This is a direct parallel to the story of Abraham, who also finds out about the impending birth of his son Isaac through the visit of angels. Gabriel tells Zechariah the name of the boy and gives notice of the joy and gladness that will accompany his birth. But Zechariah doubts this news, and in response, the angel makes him mute until the birth of his son. It seems Zechariah needs to learn some kind of lesson about trust! Zechariah is forced to listen and doesn't utter a word for nine months. At the end of this time, Zechariah regains his voice (apparently he has learned his lesson) and names the newborn child John, as Gabriel has directed.

I like to believe that angels are present at the birth of every child. I remember going to the hospital on the night my first son was born. There was a full moon and I knew, I just knew, that someone incredible was coming into the world. There was something spiritual going on, a rejoicing in heaven, and I believe this kind of rejoicing happens every time a child makes his or her way into the world.

Zechariah's son, whom we come to know as John the Baptist, is unique— and not just because he wears a camel's hair cloak and eats locusts. John the Baptist is special. But so too is every human being born in the world, and I believe angels accompany the birth of each. Perhaps the newborns see the angels, and we adults are too busy with other things to notice them.

Life is holy. And when it begins, heaven touches earth. We must never forget this, no matter how much pain we have to endure or how much of a struggle life can be. Life is good. Human life is very good. And angels come to us to let us know that each human soul contains a piece of the divine spark and is a cause for joy in heaven.

Twenty

MARY'S ENCOUNTER

And [the angel Gabriel] came to her and said, "Greetings, favored one! The Lord is with you." But she was much perplexed by his words and pondered what sort of greeting this might be. The angel said to her, "Do not be afraid, Mary, for you have found favor with God.

Luke 1:28-30

Mary is distressed—*perplexed*—by the visit of the angel. The word used here in the original language of the gospels literally means to stir up like a pot of water that begins to boil. Mary's peaceful and placid countenance is troubled. She is thrown off guard, confused, scared. Her mind is stirred and running a mile a minute. This angelic visit really shakes her up.

Luke writes that she was troubled by "what sort of greeting this might be." It is as if she has anticipated being asked a great question or given a great assignment. In other words, Mary already knows this visit is going to turn her life upside down. She just knows. This is the beginning of a new life for her. Everything is going to change.

And so it is with angels: They come to change our lives. They tell us to be not afraid while bearing the kind of news that honestly is good reason for a little fear. Their news will transform everything. The angels come in cosmic shifts, spiritual earthquakes that change the ground upon which we stand; they come in wind and fire to alter the very substance of our lives. And Mary knows this. She is stirred up and turned upside down immediately. She seems to know that this greeting will be like none other. It will change her life forever.

Mary is not asked if this is okay with her. She is not given a proposal or a suggestion. She is told by the angel that she has been selected. It is not an option or invitation. It is who she is, the favored one of God. The angel edifies and praises her but with that praise comes the hardest assignment in all of human history—to parent the incarnation of God.

When an angel appears to a human being in scripture, they often edify that person. I believe this continues today, with angels both building us up and challenging us. I guess the two go together—the edification and the challenge. Angels nudge us to grow and encourage us as we take the first step. They are catalysts for spiritual growth and development. Their visits are so rare and so potent, like a small drop of concentrated juice in a glass of water, that their presence stirs us up, permeates everything, and transforms our lives from that day forward.

The angel visits. And Mary's life is changed forever.

Gabriel & the Annunciation

Gabriel is one of only three angels named in the New Testament. In Hebrew tradition, Gabriel is a guardian angel of Israel, but in Christian tradition, he is preeminently the messenger of God to Mary, announcing the miraculous incarnation of Christ through Mary's conception. In this role, from guardian of Israel to messenger of the coming of Christ, Gabriel represents the turning from old to new, from the law of Moses to the new law of Christ, from Adam, whose sin exposed us to death, to Christ, the new Adam, whose coming sacrifice promises redemption and life.

The annunciation has been depicted thousands of times over the centuries, in precious illuminated manuscripts and prayer books, painted and sculpted altarpieces, humble devotional prints, and many other forms. The subject itself is very simple—the angel speaks to the young woman, Mary—but its artistic and symbolic variations and subtleties are many.

In a beautifully illuminated fifteenth-century book of hours from France (Fig. 20), the angel Gabriel approaches from the left and, kneeling, raises one hand in speech as if to attract Mary's attention. A scroll winds and twists in the air against the patterned background of the image. It is a medieval "speech bubble," inscribed with the words of Gabriel in Scripture, *Ave gratia plena,* "Hail full of grace, the Lord is with thee" (Luke 1:28). Mary is kneeling at a lectern, facing away from the angel but turns to look over her shoulder at the announcing angel. She has been praying, and the angel's entrance has interrupted her devotions. A tall white lily with three flowers rises out of a pot on the floor at the back of the room. The lily, symbol of virginity, appears in almost every

Fig. 20

image of the annunciation. The flowers here, two open and one closed, symbolize the Trinity and the coming of Christ, who soon will bloom forth as a child from Mary's womb, represented by the pot. At the top of the image, God the Father appears surrounded by a ring of seraphs and cherubs that remind us as viewers that we are now gazing from earth into heaven, as the dove of the Holy Spirit descends in the form of pure, heavenly light from God toward Mary.

Mary is depicted in devotion in this image, as she often is, and in this medieval prayer book, the image of Mary is associated with a prayer, with a verse from the Psalms (50:17), *Domine, labia mea aperies*, "O Lord, thou wilt open my lips: and my mouth shall declare thy praise." This text beneath the image is for us, the viewers, to speak in our own prayerful devotions, but the words take on special meaning in the context of Mary's story. When the angel Gabriel appears suddenly in her home and tells the young, unmarried woman that she has been chosen to bear the child of God, Mary is both frightened and embarrassed. We can well imagine her feelings. She is overwhelmed. The Bible tells us of her response: "But she was much perplexed by his words and pondered what sort of greeting this might be." The angel reassured her, "Do not be afraid Mary, for you have found favor with God." It can be hard to see some events in life as blessings, especially when they come with challenges or trials or when we wonder if we are really up to the task or capable of doing what life demands and what God asks of us. The prayer—"Open my lips"—is a prayer for the grace that Mary shows in accepting the challenge and blessing that God has brought her. In other words, we are saying, *"God, give me the strength to accept, to live up to, and to honor your blessings."*

Mary is thus a model for the viewer and the owner of this prayer book, both a model for how we, in strange providence, still honor God and for how we embrace humility and acknowledge our own sins and imperfections. Mary is regarded as the most perfect of women, yet she does not see herself this way. When the angel speaks to her, Mary is "perplexed." Medieval commentators on the Bible compare this passage of scripture to another passage from the Psalms, from the penitential Psalm 6: "Have pity on me LORD, for I am weak…my spirit shakes with terror." In this light, interpreters of the Bible consider Mary's response not only a sign of fear but also a sign of penitence, of humility.

Fig. 21

Other images of the annunciation introduce different spiritual ideas. An early Renaissance altarpiece from Italy depicts Gabriel and Mary in two separate wings (Fig. 21), the pinnacles of a larger altarpiece. Gabriel kneels before Mary, who is seated now, enthroned. She raises her right hand in a gesture of acknowledgement and holds a copy of the scriptures in her left hand over her belly. This image of Mary is a symbolic type known as the "Throne of Wisdom." It refers to the words and the spiritual meaning of John 1:1, "In the beginning was the Word, and the Word was with God, and the Word was God." Christ as the Word incarnate is symbolized by the scriptures placed over the Virgin's womb.

Representations or allusions to the Ten Commandments appear in many images, as in a seventeenth-century engraving by Hendrik Goltzius (Fig. 22), in which the Ten Commandments appear in the background.

Fig. 22

The incarnation of Christ represents the fulfillment of the old law of Moses and coming of the new law of Christ. In a German painting of the annunciation from the fifteenth century (Fig. 23), the angel Gabriel presents Mary with a document bearing three wax seals, just like a legal document of the period. This is a contract, symbolizing the new covenant, making official the law of Christ.

In many depictions of the annunciation, the angel Gabriel is remarkable for his physical presence. He is perhaps the most human looking angel in all of art, in the sense that he is not ethereal but rather large, kneeling on the ground, and heavy of body. In a Renaissance painting by Gerard David (Fig. 24), the artist depicts Gabriel and Mary as living statues, standing in niches in a wall, symbolizing their physical, embodied presence in the earthly world.

One of the most famous paintings of the annunciation (Fig. 25), a work known as the Merode Altarpiece, depicts Gabriel as a deeply physical presence. He enters into Mary's house through a door, watched

Fig. 23

Fig. 24

Fig 25

prayerfully by the human donors in the garden outside, who gave the altarpiece. Gabriel is rooted to the ground, and his wings, stirring the air, extinguish a nearby candle and cause the pages of an open book to rustle and turn. This mundane physicality is also symbolic. We are "turning the page," so to speak from the Old Testament to the New. The candle goes but the light of Christ enters into the world. Gabriel's physicality embodies and affirms the carnal truth of the incarnation and of Christ's humanity. We share in that humanity, in that perfect imperfection, to which the images of Gabriel and Mary give both real form and spiritual meaning.

Twenty-One

DREAMS

Her husband Joseph, being a righteous man and unwilling to expose her to public disgrace, planned to dismiss her quietly. But just when he had resolved to do this, an angel of the Lord appeared to him in a dream and said, "Joseph, son of David, do not be afraid to take Mary as your wife, for the child conceived in her is from the Holy Spirit. She will bear a son and you will name him Jesus, for he will save the people from their sins."

Matthew 1:19-21

Why do we dream? I think most of the time we dream to process all that our minds have observed and felt and experienced. I dream anxious dreams when I am under stress. Just two nights ago I dreamed that I left dirty laundry in the sanctuary of our church and had to rush to pick it up before the service began. That kind of dream is my mind processing: Perhaps it was the four loads of laundry I did for my husband and boys or the fact that I worry about not being prepared for worship. Who knows, exactly. Yet listening to our dreams can be a fascinating window into our mental processing.

Occasionally some of us experience what I'll call "God dreams." They don't come from some deep-seated anxiety or the leftover morphing of a movie or book; rather, they come from an outside source. My friend dreamed that she was walking down an aisle as a bride and when she looked up, she saw Jesus was the groom. These dreams change us. These dreams do not fade as quickly as we wipe the sleep from our eyes. They stay vivid and clear even years later. I suppose that anything that comes from the great I AM does not exist in time as we know it and cannot be forgotten. This type of dream seems to imprint permanently on our minds.

Joseph has such a dream. He knows the dream is not a figment of his own mind. He had been afraid to take the already-pregnant Mary as his wife, but in the dream, an angel tells him not to be afraid, that this marriage is God's plan and a son will be born, a son who is from God.

It is hard to imagine what would have happened if Joseph hadn't listened to his dream. He might not have taken Mary as his wife. As a pregnant woman without a husband, she might have been stoned to death. Then Jesus would not have been born. And the world as we know it would not be the same. It is incredible to ponder the importance of this dream—and not only the dream but also the importance of Joseph's response. He listens. He obeys. He may not understand, but he marries this young pregnant girl—against the advice of every sensible person in Nazareth, no doubt. Joseph decides to listen to a dream and accept its truth. Thank God for that.

Twenty-Two

ANGELS IN THE SKY

In that region there were shepherds living in the fields, keeping watch over their flock by night. Then an angel of the Lord stood before them, and the glory of the Lord shone around them, and they were terrified. But the angel said to them, "Do not be afraid; for see—I am bringing you good news of great joy for all the people: to you is born this day in the city of David a Savior, who is the Messiah, the Lord."
Luke 2:8-11

This morning I walked my dogs as the sun was rising. As usual, I was consumed with all the things I had to do today and all the mistakes I made the day before. Things done and left undone, as the confession states. And, as usual, I felt overwhelmed.

The sun rose over the river, turning the sky to a shade of pink. And I started to breathe deeply. "Beautiful," I thought. And then some kind thoughts filled my mind, thoughts of such love and forgiveness for myself and others. I knew these thoughts were a gift, an angelic kiss, so to speak. They were new and so very kind. I no longer felt overwhelmed but full of joy.

I believe it is easier to experience the presence of the angelic influence when we are outside in nature. The beauty of creation opens our hearts, making us more receptive to good news, and pulls us out of the morass of our worries and into a longing for the Creator.

The shepherds live outside. As caretakers for their animals, they are forced to sleep outdoors. In Bethlehem, sheep graze at night because the days can be too hot. So the shepherds find themselves wandering the hillsides at night and sleeping in caves with their sheep in the heat of the day. They walk the hills counting the sheep and the stars, witnessing the beauty of the night sky.

In this setting, the angels come and deliver a birth announcement. It reminds me of the official in London who stood outside the hospital and announced the birth of a royal son born to William and Kate. These angels proclaim the birth of royalty, cosmic royalty, so their announcement is made from the stars. *To you is born this day*, they say. *To you.* Christ is born to you and to me and to all of us. He is ours forever: He belongs to the shepherds and the poor and the weak and to me and to you. He belongs to all of us.

Step outside. Look around. Breathe. If you want to be open to the visit of angels, I think outside is the best place to be.

Twenty-Three

ANGELS' ABSENCE

Now when all the people were baptized and when Jesus also had been baptized, and was praying, the heaven was opened, and the Holy Spirit descended upon him in bodily form like a dove. And a voice came from heaven, "You are my Son, the Beloved; with you I am well pleased."

Luke 3:21-22

It must seem strange to read a meditation about the absence of angels, but I think it is significant that there are no angels described as being present at the baptism of Jesus. Unlike the birth narratives, which are written in only two of the four gospels, the story of Jesus' baptism is present in all four gospel accounts. Clearly it is a pivotal moment in the life of Jesus. It is the moment when he comes into his fullness. There is no record of Jesus as an adult doing anything at all until after he is baptized. It is almost as if he is not fully alive until that moment.

For Christians, life with God begins at baptism. It is when we are invited to awaken to who we really are. So why aren't angels present?

One thing I have learned in my twenty years as a priest is that my absence can be as powerful and as significant as my presence. We are baptizing four children tomorrow (it is the Feast of the Baptism of Jesus). At the rehearsal today, I spoke to the parents and godparents about the meaning of baptism and how to care for and nurture the spiritual lives of their children. At the end of the rehearsal, I suggested that they spend about fifteen minutes getting to know each other. After all, they are to become god brothers and sisters. And then, I left, on purpose.

I find that when I am present, people don't bond like they should. Community is sometimes better built when the leader steps away. I needed to give them room to talk to each other. And they did.

Perhaps angels withheld their presence from the baptism of Jesus because it was a moment for God to connect directly with Jesus and with all of humanity. This is a moment when a direct interaction takes place between the Almighty and the Incarnation.

The Holy Spirit descends directly upon Jesus and in some gospel accounts is visible to everyone present. Some say the Spirit looks like a dove. And God speaks. God talks directly not just to Jesus but in range of the entire company. The only other moment that God directly addresses humans is on the mountain during the Transfiguration. This conversation at Jesus' baptism is a direct encounter. There are no messengers, no intermediaries, not even an angelic cheering section (at least not one that is visible). This is between God and humankind.

It is strange that angels are there at the birth of Jesus and at the resurrection but not at his baptism. But maybe they knew that God needed to make it clear whose son Jesus is. And whose children we are.

Twenty-Four

THE DEVIL

Jesus, full of the Holy Spirit, returned from the Jordan and was led by the Spirit in the wilderness, where for forty days he was tempted by the devil.

Luke 4:1-2a

One cannot talk about angels without mentioning the devil. This one goes by many names: Satan, Lucifer, the Beast. If angels are part of the vast array of God's creation, then they too are free to love and, if free to love, then free to choose to hate as well. The devil is that anti-angel, the inevitable result of true freedom. An angel of the highest order, he chose to defy God and fell from God's presence. Instead of loving and edifying, the devil's sole purpose is to bring darkness, chaos, doubt, and despair. Quite simply, he is hatred personified.

Jesus deliberately faces the devil immediately after his baptism and before he does anything else. This is a wonderful example for all humanity, for we cannot serve God until we can distinguish between God's voice and the voice of the devil. All of us, even Jesus, must listen to the voice of this dark one; he questions all of us, even in the Garden of Eden.

So Jesus listens as the devil tempts him. Jesus refuses each of the three temptations, but even after the struggle is over and Jesus remains standing and the angels come to wait on him, Luke includes a very important phrase. He writes, "When the devil had finished every test, he departed from him until an opportune time" (4:13). It is clear, even in the case of the Son of God, that the devil will return. The devil will not leave us; he will not give up until this human life has ended. And as an angel himself, the devil is immortal. He does not tire; he will not wear out. So we had better get to know his voice.

All human beings are tempted. We hear the voices of inner criticism, hatred, and despair almost constantly. Our job is to identify these temptations placed there by the devil and to bring them into the light. Darkness cannot withstand light and truth.

Do you know the landscape of your own mind?[8] The devil, unlike the other angels, intrudes and does not wait for an invitation to begin speaking. Instead of saying, "Do not be afraid," the devil implores us to be frightened, to be terrified, to become paralyzed by our fear. Fear is the devil's concubine, and she loves him dearly. Panic, anxiety, stress, alienation: these are all the tools of his trade. Know them well, learn to identify their insipid intrusion, as they are on the side of darkness.

If we are to contemplate the existence of angels, there is no avoiding this dark one. But the devil is not God; he is no match for the Creator. He is no match for the Light.

Twenty-Five

Temptation and the Good News

Jesus said to him, "Away with you Satan! for it is written, 'Worship the Lord your God, and serve only him.'"
Then the devil left him, and suddenly angels came and waited on him.

Matthew 4:10-11

Angels appear far more often in the New Testament than in the Old Testament. Angels bring good news. Angels are signs of God's presence and communication with us, and when Jesus comes, the appearance of angels increases. Communication with God increases, and angels come around more often, particularly at the pivotal events of his life.

The gospels are full of a certain kind of paradigm: Demons are cast out, and angels come in. Angels appear at the birth of Jesus, they minister to him after the temptation, they comfort him in Gethsemane, and they witness the resurrection. Demons are present only in broken human beings, and the devil himself tempts Jesus but fails to convince him to sin. The good guys win. They always win when it comes to Jesus and the good news.

When I watch TV, I feel like our world is falling apart. Our government is bitterly divided. Challenges from China, North Korea, and Russia are daunting. People are starving, and refugees are fleeing war-torn countries. Just read the newspapers. It feels like the news is almost all bad. And yet, in her article "Five graphs that will change your mind about poverty," Chelsea Follet writes, "Indeed, of those rare people who realize that extreme poverty has declined, almost all underestimate the extent of that decline. In fact, global poverty has halved over the past twenty years—but only one person in 100 gets it right."[9]

Why do we not talk more about this good news? Why are we so prone today to focus on the negative?

As people of the Good News of Christ, it is our job and vocation to keep the bad news in perspective. Should we strive to alleviate suffering and end violence throughout the world? Yes! But we must celebrate each tiny child who is born into love and honor each meal that is prepared with care. We must not take for granted what we have been given and how far we have come. Often our greatest lessons happen when we make our biggest mistakes. There are angels around, and there is good news. Don't forget to look for both!

I am convinced that our perception is directly influenced by our choices. Will you choose to dwell on the negative or celebrate what is good? The choice is up to you. Certainly, we must observe the world with clear eyes and address the pain and suffering in the world, but we must not fail to notice and give thanks for the good things in life. We can find angels or demons in our lives at almost all times. Each one of us can choose to focus on one or the other, to give our attention to one or the other. Which will it be? And the more that we look, the more we will see. The spiritual world waits for us to open our eyes and see.

Twenty-Six

STIRRING UP

Now in Jerusalem by the Sheep Gate there is a pool, called in Hebrew Beth-zatha, which has five porticoes. In these lay many invalids—blind, lame, and paralyzed. **For an angel of the Lord went down at certain seasons into the pool and stirred up the water; whoever stepped in first, after the stirring of the water, was made well from whatever disease with which he was afflicted.**

John 5:2-4

Verse four of this gospel passage is in bold type to indicate that most Bibles leave it out. There is some debate about why this has happened. Biblical scholars research when verses of manuscripts contradict each other or when some are omitted. In this case, since the bulk of the manuscripts seem to have omitted this sentence about angels, most Bibles now jump from verse three to verse five and simply leave out the angels.

Why the discrepancy? Certainly, the missing verse makes the story much more colorful, explaining why those who were sick or suffering would sit in the pool all day. An angel stirring up the pool sounds marvelous to me. But was it just the hope and the tales of the sick or did an angel actually appear? Jesus does come and heal them, so in a sense, he becomes their angel. So is it all that important to know if *at certain seasons* an angel visited them or not?

The angel in this passage is not a biblical certainty; rather he or she is a biblical possibility. In his book *Walking in Wonder,* author John O'Donohue writes, "Possibilities are always more interesting than facts. We shouldn't frown on facts, but our world is congested with them.

Facts are retarded possibilities; they are possibilities that have already been actualized."[10] The angel that stirred up the water was added later in scripture, it is true, but the echo of this angel's presence speaks to us now, even if it is only an idea, a possibility.

I can picture the sick and the lame, in pain and misery, soaking in these waters and waiting for a cool breeze to come and break the heat of the Middle East. And who is to say if that breeze did not carry with it an invisible angel and a healing touch? It seems to me that the possibility of an angelic presence in the gentle breeze or the stirring wind is always present to us. There have been times when I have felt caressed by the wind, touched and loved. The word for spirit in the ancient Hebrew, *ruach*, is the same as the word for wind. Why do we so often deny the possibility that they are both present in the breeze, the life of the Spirit and the simple moving of air molecules? I want to reclaim the possibility that an angel stirs the water and brings healing. I want to imagine it.

Twenty-Seven

GETHSEMANE

Then he withdrew from them about a stone's throw, knelt down, and prayed, "Father, if you are willing, remove this cup from me; yet, not my will but yours be done." Then an angel from heaven appeared to him and gave him strength. In his anguish he prayed more earnestly, and his sweat became like great drops of blood falling down on the ground.
Luke 22:41-44

When Jesus is sitting in the garden of Gethsemane, terrified of the agony that awaits him, an angel appears to him and gives him strength. The angel does not make the situation go away; she does not fix the horror that is to come. She simply stays with Jesus. The angel's presence gives Jesus strength even in the midst of his agony.

Angels encourage, but they do not enable. They do not rescue a person but can help them endure what they must, to find the strength that they need. On a recent visit to a rehabilitation center, I saw a handsome young man adeptly assist an elderly man who was recovering from a stroke. The young man was a speech therapist, and he really knew what he was doing. He could not speak for the elderly man or take away the despair the man was feeling at the loss of his speech. But the therapist could instruct and encourage. He would challenge the elderly man with a word, and when the man made an attempt, the therapist cheered. Every drool, mumble, puff, and blow were met with a smile and encouragement.

We are all stumbling about in this life, terrified and inadequate most of the time. The angels cannot live our lives for us nor can they fix the messes that we encounter (or are of our own making), but they can cheer for us, they can inspire us, and they can love us no matter what. They can sing to us and smile at us and be our loudest cheering section.

I remember watching the end of an Ironman triathlon. After 2.4 miles of swimming, a 112-mile bicycle ride, and a marathon run, the competitors were physically and mentally depleted. Some could hardly walk. And yet the crowd began to scream and cheer as soon as one of them neared the finish line. We hollered and stamped our feet, and it seemed that the sheer force of our enthusiasm gave them strength to finish.

Angels are not there to live our lives or fix things that are broken. But they are present on the sidelines cheering for you. And when you stumble, they cheer harder. They comforted Jesus when he felt despair, and they will do the same for you now.

Twenty-Eight

EASTER ANGELS

And very early on the first day of the week, when the sun had risen, they went to the tomb. They had been saying to one another, "Who will roll away the stone for us from the entrance to the tomb?" When they looked up, they saw that the stone, which was very large, had already been rolled back. As they entered the tomb, they saw a young man, dressed in a white robe, sitting on the right side; and they were alarmed. But he said to them, "Do not be alarmed; you are looking for Jesus of Nazareth, who was crucified. He has been raised; he is not here. Look, there is the place they laid him. But go, tell his disciples and Peter that he is going ahead of you to Galilee; there you will see him, just as he told you." So they went out and fled from the tomb, for terror and amazement had seized them; and they said nothing to anyone, for they were afraid.

Mark 16:2-8

All four gospel accounts mention a man (or sometimes two) dressed in white standing in or near the tomb. In Mark and in Luke, these angels passively sit at the scene ready to give an account of what Jesus has done. In Matthew, the angel moves the stone away from the tomb and overwhelms the disciples with his light. Scripture is clear that angels were present at the tomb, but why were they there?

Just like at the birth of Jesus, something happens in the event of the resurrection that breaks the earthly mold. The resurrection event is so inconceivable that it needs a translator, a messenger to explain to the disciples what has occurred. *He is not here; he has risen!*

I am convinced that every spark of innovation, every truly new idea, comes from God through the Holy Spirit—and often the ones to carry that inspiration are the angels. We need translators and interpreters to help us understand that a man who was dead is now alive. Someone has to spell it out for us. Otherwise, we will never be able to take it in. Someone has to make sure the message actually enters our minds and sticks there!

And we need angels for this very reason today. More than 2,000 years after the resurrection, we are still trying to comprehend it. The resurrection changes everything about the way we view the world and our lives and the life to come. We need help understanding its message, even as it still unfolds today.

He is not here. We are looking in the wrong place. He is more than a dead body, so much more. We must look for him in ourselves, in the places and people we love, in each other. The angels say this, and the disciples have no idea what they mean. We still have no idea what the words actually mean, but we are trying to understand.

Heaven touches earth at these moments of incomprehensibility and genuine wonder. Angels touch us.

Last night, there was a super moon, or a blood moon as some call it. At 1:40 a.m., I awoke with a start and rushed outside into the cold winter air to see it. I could see such light; it illumined my entire backyard. The moon was so bright that I could see the craters on its surface. Who woke me up? My internal clock is just not that good.

"Wake up," the angels often say. They are interpreting for God, who reminds us that the universe is so much larger than we think. *Listen, look, take in the light, and learn something new. If the light is too bright for you, I will share it with you in small increments. I will send my messengers to spell it out for you until you can conceive of and accept this transformative love.*

Twenty-Nine

MOVING STONES, SHAKING THE EARTH

After the sabbath, as the first day of the week was dawning, Mary Magdalene and the other Mary went to see the tomb. And suddenly there was a great earthquake; for an angel of the Lord, descending from heaven, came and rolled back the stone and sat on it. His appearance was like lightning, and his clothing white as snow. For fear of him the guards shook and became like dead men. But the angel said to the women, "Do not be afraid; I know that you are looking for Jesus who was crucified. He is not here; for he has been raised, as he said. Come, see the place where he lay. Then go quickly and tell his disciples, 'He has been raised from the dead, and indeed he is going ahead of you to Galilee; there you will see him.' This is my message for you."

Matthew 28:1-7

Angels appear at the tomb in all four gospel accounts, but only in Matthew does the angel express himself in events of nature and make such a physical impression on the earth itself. This angel descends bodily from heaven, shakes the earth as he rolls back the immense stone that stood before the tomb, and takes on the appearance of lightning. It is as if this angel is harnessing the power of the natural world to express the victory of the resurrection. And it is a mighty scene indeed.

Does nature reflect the events of the spiritual world? Does the natural world respond to the birth of Jesus and to his resurrection? According to Matthew, angels relate to the natural world in the time of Christ.

They come to us in solid forms to roll away stones, shake the earth, and give off flashes of light. They are physical beings, strong, mighty, and expressive.

Indeed, Matthew describes the earth roiling in pain and shaking when Jesus dies on the cross. Physical things happen in the natural world to express the grief and pain of God: an earthquake, a curtain being torn in two, and darkness covering the land. Matthew sees all of nature as expressing the love of God, and in that way, nature becomes a kind of angel or messenger unto itself.

If Matthew is right and angels do express themselves through natural events, then we must view the earth itself as a source of wisdom and expression from God. Saint Francis viewed nature in this way. He believed that all events of nature were lessons or messages from God, from how the birds lived their lives in song and praise to the way rains fed the earth to produce food for us to eat. Francis saw all of nature as a messenger or a transmitter of God's love. Even the animals were like angels to Francis, teaching us how to live lives of freedom and joy.

Indeed, if an angel is a messenger from God and God as Creator can express love through the natural world, then all of God's creation can become like the angels, bringing us something from God, something for us to learn and understand, an expression of the great joy and love of the Creator for all of this creation.

Thirty

CONNECTING THE DOTS

They found the stone rolled away from the tomb, but when they went in, they did not find the body. While they were perplexed about this, suddenly two men in dazzling clothes stood beside them. The women were terrified and bowed their faces to the ground, but the men said to them, "Why do you look for the living among the dead? He is not here but has risen. Remember how he told you, while he was still in Galilee, that the Son of Man must be handed over to sinners, and be crucified, and on the third day rise again." Then they remembered his words, and returning from the tomb, they told all this to the eleven and to all the rest.

Luke 24:2-9

This time Luke describes the messengers as men dressed in dazzling clothes. The adjective translated as dazzling is also used to describe the radiance of Jesus, Moses, and Elijah at the mountain of the Transfiguration. It is light from heaven, brighter than any radiance we have ever seen on earth.

The women are confused, and the angels bring them clarity by reminding them of what they already know, reminding them of Jesus' words to them. The pieces of a broken puzzle seem to come together in the minds of these women as these angels speak to them. The women move from fear and grief to joy and understanding. They remember and with that memory comes understanding.

I wonder if angels are moving in the mind of my mathematician friend who will go to sleep with an unsolved problem on his mind, and somewhere in the midst of the night, he awakens to understand. He describes this phenomenon as being like when the pieces of a puzzle come together. Could it be that he is touched by wisdom from heaven, by some kind of heavenly messenger? These "aha" moments are gifts, moments when everything becomes simple and clear. It all makes sense.

Remember, they say. Remember Jesus' words to you. Remember who he is and who you are. You know the truth; just find it within yourself.

Sometimes we need a little help connecting the dots, putting it all together. Perhaps the angels are the ones who open our minds to what we already know. *Remember*, they say. Remember.

Thirty-One

Looking in the Wrong Place

But Mary stood weeping outside the tomb. As she wept, she bent over to look into the tomb; and she saw two angels in white, sitting where the body of Jesus had been lying, one at the head and the other at the feet. They said to her, "Woman, why are you weeping?" She said to them, "They have taken away my Lord, and I do not know where they have laid him." When she had said this, she turned around and saw Jesus standing there.

John 20:11-14

In the Gospel of John, both the angels and Jesus ask Mary Magdalene the very same question: "Woman, why are you weeping?" First, the angels appear and pose this question, then comes the Risen Christ. There is something significant about this question.

Perhaps the angels and Jesus know that in order for Mary to see the Risen Christ, she must first listen to herself and understand her own pain. I find it remarkable that in the midst of the incredible news of the resurrection, the angels first stop to listen to Mary and to acknowledge her suffering. They see her crying, and they remark upon it. They let her experience her feelings first before showing her the Lord. They let her cry.

Asking this question illustrates the love that both the angels and Jesus feel for Mary. They truly want to know why she is in pain. They do not gloss over her tears or belittle them by launching into their joyful announcement; they stop to notice and to speak to her, to listen to her response. She is heard; her pain is acknowledged.

Mary explains that she is crying because they have taken away her Lord. Jesus does not then tell her she is mistaken or her feelings are invalid: He simply says her name, and Mary recognizes that Jesus is in fact standing before her.

Sometimes we must move through our tears to find joy. My husband is a psychotherapist. His practice is based on the premise that human beings need to be heard. Often people will move through their own pain and find light on the other side simply by being in the presence of people who sincerely care and who lovingly ask why they are crying.

Thirty-Two

THE ASCENSION

As they were watching, he was lifted up, and a cloud took him out of their sight. While he was going and they were gazing up toward heaven, suddenly two men in white robes stood by them. They said, "Men of Galilee, why do you stand looking up towards heaven? This Jesus, who has been taken up from you into heaven, will come in the same way as you saw him go into heaven."

Acts 1:9-11

Just as they are present at the tomb after the resurrection, so the two men of Luke's Gospel appear again as Jesus leaves for good. At the scene of the resurrection, the two men ask the women, "Why do you look for the living among the dead?" and here at the departure of Jesus, they ask a similar question, "Why do you stand looking up towards heaven?" The angels want both the women and the disciples to look for God's activity here on earth, to focus on this life.

We have already seen that one of the purposes of angels is to wake us up. As humans, we benignly and gently become spiritually and emotionally unconscious, until we are nudged awake. I will be driving my car, zoning out to who knows what on the radio, when a startling sunset will wake me up and I remember to thank God for the day. I will be in a store when I glance up and see a friend who has just been on my mind. When I am musing about a sermon, my eyes will fall on relevant books and articles, addressing the very ideas that were formulating in my mind. Are these mere coincidences? Or might this be the work of angels nudging me, hoping I will wake up and see their loving hands at work in the world?

I used to love hiding Easter eggs for my boys when they were little. My husband and I would have so much fun placing them in obvious places for the youngest and challenging the oldest to look harder for the ones that were truly hidden. We felt such joy when they found those candy eggs. It was so much fun!

I think angels take this same delight as we search and find God's hand at work in the world. As Christians we are ultimately waiting for Christ to come again, but this kind of waiting takes practice. In the meantime, we need the equivalent of Easter egg hunts, moments where we actively seek grace, beauty, and meaning. Angels lead us to search in the right places, just as I would stand near an Easter egg and giggle as my boys ran to me and looked around eagerly. "Look!" they say. Look for God's Spirit. Look for God's goodness. Look for God's love. It is all around you.

Thirty-Three

RELEASE FROM PRISON

Then the high priest took action; he and all who were with him (that is, the sect of the Sadducees), being filled with jealousy, arrested the apostles and put them in the public prison. But during the night an angel of the Lord opened the prison doors, brought them out, and said, "Go, stand in the temple and tell the people the whole message about this life." When they heard this, they entered the temple at daybreak and went on with their teaching.

Acts 5:17-21a

An angel releases the apostles from prison. This kind of miraculous intervention happens a lot in the Book of Acts. Angels are all over the place, taking a very active role in the life of the early church and rescuing the apostles from some dangerous situations. It reminds me of how I used to push my boys on their three-wheel bicycles before they got the hang of pedaling themselves. I nudged and prodded and pushed them forward until they could ride on their own. In these passages of scripture, it is as if the angels are saying, "Oh, he needs a push here! Oh, let's get those folks out of prison…" The angels act as catalysts in the initial spreading of the gospel until the early Christians get their feet under them and get moving on their own power. Then the angels step back a bit.

In the passage above, an angel appears and simply opens the doors of the prison. It seems the angel is adept at freeing prisoners. I believe this is still the case, not just for the early apostles but also for prisoners today. If we are willing to turn our lives to God, release from prison is possible, and angels will help us.

Khalil Osiris[11] was imprisoned for twenty years. Inside those walls he found freedom, inner freedom, which Khalil says is much more important than physical freedom—and much harder to find. Khalil's angel took the form of a judge who, at his second sentencing, said to him, "Young man, you could be sitting in the attorney's chair. You could be sitting in my seat, but you chose to commit a crime. Yes, you may have been angry and maybe someone wronged you or you think you deserve to take what is not yours, but you chose crime and now you are reaping the results of your choice. Remember that you are free to choose between right and wrong. That choice is always yours, whether you are in prison or out."

Khalil heard the judge. He could have rejected this invitation or reacted in anger. He could have railed against the injustice of it all, but he chose to accept the challenge and acknowledge the freedoms that he did have. And from that point, jail became his university. He was free to get a bachelor's degree, and then a master's. He emerged from prison a new man, a passionate preacher and teacher. He found freedom inside jail. In fact, his freedom had very little to do with the bars of his cell and everything to do with his mindset.

Angels invite all of us to be free: free from resentment and anger, free from carrying the burdens of grudges or hatred. They invite us to forgive. When we carry resentment, the burden is like a great boulder, weighing us down, keeping us from becoming all that God has called us to be. Forgiveness is not about feeling warm and fuzzy or condoning bad behavior. It is about letting go of that which is keeping us in bondage. It is about freedom. And the angels want to set us free so that we can do the work that God has called us to do.

Thirty-Four

CORNELIUS

In Caesarea there was a man named Cornelius, a centurion of the Italian Cohort, as it was called. He was a devout man who feared God with all his household; he gave alms generously to the people and prayed constantly to God. One afternoon at about three o'clock he had a vision in which he clearly saw an angel of God coming in and saying to him, "Cornelius." He stared at him in terror and said, "What is it, Lord?" He answered, "Your prayers and your alms have ascended as a memorial before God. Now send men to Joppa for a certain Simon who is called Peter; he is lodging with Simon, a tanner, whose house is by the seaside." When the angel who spoke to him had left, he called two of his slaves and a devout soldier from the ranks of those who served him, and after telling them everything, he sent them to Joppa.

Acts 10:1-8

Why do so many Americans purchase statues and cards that depict fat baby angels? There is no way angels look like this! Almost every time angels appear in scripture, they instill fear. Not once in all of the Bible does someone encounter an angel and exclaim, "Oh, how cute!" or "Let me hold you!" No, people are terrified when they see angels because often, they are described as fiery creatures that arouse awe, fear, and reverence.

Here is Cornelius, a centurion, a Roman soldier in charge of one-hundred men, and he stares in terror at the angel. Cornelius is, presumably, a brave man, one who has seen war and commanded soldiers. And he is struck dumb, not just with fear but also terror. He calls the angel, "Lord," not "sweetie pie" or "cutie." Let's get rid of the image of the cupid-baby as angel. It's an insult to the heavenly host.

Later in the Book of Acts, we hear about the first major dispute of the early church. This dispute centers on the inclusion of the Gentiles. Does a Gentile have to become a Jew before being baptized? Jesus is Jewish but does that mean that all of his followers have to be? If a Gentile wants to become a Christian, must a man be circumcised first?

When the debate ensues, Peter recalls how an angel appears to a Gentile man, and, not just any man but a Roman soldier of some repute. The angel appears to a man who is the supposed enemy and oppressor of the believers. Why?

God does not have the borders and boundaries that we humans have adopted. For the Creator, no one is outside the gospel message; the angel's visit to Cornelius illustrates this profound truth. Angels will come where they will. We are not in control of whom God chooses, and we have no idea of how salvation actually works. All we can do is pray and open our hearts to God.

In addition, the selection of Cornelius among all other Roman centurions gives us insight into our relationship with God. While Cornelius is not yet a follower of Christ, he is nonetheless a man of prayer, one who fears God, as the scripture says. Further, the author of Luke and Acts describes Cornelius's generosity in giving money to the poor—even before telling of his prayer practice.

Do you want to see angels? Given how scary they seem to be, I am not always sure. But if the answer is yes, then I must learn to give even before I pray. And I must be ready for something terrifying and beautiful and life changing.

Thirty-Five

FERVENT PRAYER

While Peter was kept in prison, the church prayed fervently to God for him. The very night before Herod was going to bring him out, Peter, bound with two chains, was sleeping between two soldiers, while guards in front of the door were keeping watch over the prison. Suddenly an angel of the Lord appeared and a light shone in the cell. He tapped Peter on the side and woke him, saying, "Get up quickly." And the chains fell off his wrists.

Acts 12:5-7

An angel escorts Peter out of prison. Peter is in chains, he is in a cell, surrounded by guards, and he still is led to freedom. It is nothing short of miraculous. When he arrives at his friends' home and knocks on the door, they simply can't believe their eyes.

All this happens while the church is praying for Peter. And they are not just praying, but praying *fervently*. The ancient Greek word for this kind of prayer means to pray intently and without stopping. The early church makes this kind of prayer a priority. They don't just mention Peter in their prayers: they focus on him and bring his needs to God over and over and over again. And the result is the visitation of an angel.

Prayer does change things. When I say I will pray for someone, I often feel a great sense of both responsibility and inadequacy. To truly pray for others means not just mentioning them to God but holding them in a kind of embrace before God—and coming back to that embrace over and over again. This kind of prayer can truly release people from prison and bring about miracles, but this fervent prayer is intense and requires work.

I can picture the early Christians kneeling together in secret and praying with earnest hope and fear for Peter. Will he be put to death? Will he be tortured? In total helplessness, they reach out to God and ask God to embrace Peter and to free him from captivity. And when Peter shows up the next night, they can't believe their eyes.

The answer to these fervent prayers is Peter's freedom. But we must remember that release from prison may not look the same for us as for Peter. God answers our prayers—and sometimes angels bring us that response—but the response may surprise us, leading us to places we would never go or carrying us to discover new answers.

Ultimately, Peter ends up dying. But he dies in complete and utter freedom. And even in his death, his prayers and the prayers of the early Christians are answered in ways many of them—and us—cannot begin to understand.

Thirty-Six

PERSPECTIVE

When it was decided that we were to sail for Italy, they transferred Paul and some other prisoners to a centurion of the Augustan Cohort, named Julius. Embarking on a ship of Adramyttium that was about to set sail to the ports along the coast of Asia, we put to sea...Since they had been without food for a long time, Paul then stood up among them and said, "Men, you should have listened to me and not have set sail from Crete and thereby avoided this damage and loss. I urge you now to keep up your courage, for there will be no loss of life among you, but only of the ship. For last night there stood by me an angel of the God to whom I belong and whom I worship, and he said, 'Do not be afraid, Paul; you must stand before the emperor; and indeed, God has granted safety to all those who are sailing with you.' So keep up your courage, men, for I have faith in God that it will be exactly as I have been told. But we will have to run aground on some island."

Acts 27:1-2, 21-26

In the movie *The Life of Pi*, a young Indian boy appears to be the lone survivor of a sinking ship. Aboard a small boat, he survives with a tiger, and miraculously, they keep one another alive. The boy is caught in a massive storm while drifting in the small boat and in the midst of the driving rain, strong winds, and huge waves, he screams into the darkness, "I SURRENDER!"

Saul thinks he is in control of his life. He is bent on persecuting Christians and spends his days seeking them out and even watching them be stoned to death. But God transforms Saul, temporarily blinding him as a way of teaching him to surrender his will to that of Christ.

Toward the end of his ministry, Saul-now-Paul knows that God wants him to go to Rome. He boards a ship, but the waves and weather put the vessel at risk. Paul asks God for guidance, and an angel appears. The angel tells Paul not to be afraid: All aboard will survive, and Paul is destined to stand before the emperor. How does the angel know the sailors will survive and the ship will be marooned? How does the angel know that Paul is to stand before the emperor? Paul understands that the angel has a perspective that he does not.

Sometimes when I am wondering about the perspective of the angels, I picture myself watching a mouse that is making its way through a maze. I am standing above the maze, looking down on the mouse. From my perspective, I can easily tell the mouse which way to turn to make its way out of the maze (if mice could speak, of course). I can see everything. I can see what will happen to the mouse if it chooses to make this turn or that. From my vantage point above, my perspective is simple and clear.

Angels come to us from above. They transcend our simple chronological time. God can see where we are going and knows what choices will get us to where we want to be—and what choices will derail our plans. God sends angels to guide us from this heavenly perspective. We have free will. We have choices, and we don't have to follow the advice of an angel, but if we want to exit the bondage of broken living, it is wise to listen. Angels are sent from a different perspective: from the One who can see where we are going and get us to where we want to be.

Paul knows the angels see things he cannot, and he listens to them.

Thirty-Seven

An Audience of Observers

For I think that God exhibited us apostles as last of all, as though sentenced to death, because we have become a spectacle to the world, to angels and to mortals.

1 Corinthians 4:9

Paul refers to angels in this passage as if they are constantly observing the world. Paul has become a very public figure. His teachings and letters are spreading across the early churches as he travels. The Roman authorities are watching him. But for Paul, this earthly audience is nothing compared to the great numbers of angels that watch over all of us, a choir that cares deeply for all of God's creatures.[12]

I have tried throughout my life not to depend too much on the opinion of others. As someone who wanted to be an actress as a teenager and young adult, this was a hard goal. I found myself constantly analyzing the response of audiences and the feedback from people I valued. Was I known? What did people think of me? Did they like me?

I had a tendency, and perhaps you do too, to dwell on those who find fault in me and cast aside the positive opinions. Even today, I have to be careful not to let the one negative comment overshadow all the positive feedback. How do we strike a balance of listening and learning from others and being faithful to who we are and who we believe that God is calling us to be?

Jesus tells his disciples in the Gospel of Matthew that they may be hated by many at times but in the end "will be saved." Paul says God has called him to be a fool on numerous occasions, and indeed, all humanity must seem almost like a comedy of errors to the angels. We are so limited; we make such grand mistakes. And yet, we can also create spectacular beauty and perform acts of great love and kindness. If we are the performers and the angels are our audience, then I imagine a scene like two loving parents watching their young daughter in her first ballet recital. Is she silly? Yes. Does she know the steps well? Unlikely. But her parents find her incredibly beautiful and there is nowhere they would rather be than watching their daughter dance. If Paul or the early disciples obsess about the opinion of others, the work of the kingdom will never get done!

If angels are watching over us, then perhaps we should strive for their opinion. If we picture an audience of angels cheering us on, wanting the best for us and helping us find our joy, we will have the strength to receive negative feedback in a way that edifies and builds instead of tears down and destroys. How might your behavior, decisions, and thoughts change if you believe you are in the constant sight of angels?

Thirty-Eight

JUDGING ANGELS

When any of you has a grievance against another, do you dare to take it to court before the unrighteous, instead of taking it before the saints? Do you not know that the saints will judge the world? And if the world is to be judged by you, are you incompetent to try trivial cases? Do you not know that you are to judge angels—to say nothing of ordinary matters?

1 Corinthians 6:1-3

In the landscape of our minds, there are many thoughts and voices. We internalize outside sources such as the media or the advice of a loved one, but we are also heavily influenced by memory and imagination. Angels are influencers—they bring us messages. Some, as we've seen in scripture, appear as physical messengers; others are only met in dreams or visions. According to scripture, some angels give messages from God, and some, the fallen angels, influence us in ways that tend toward chaos and destruction.

Paul tells us that we will one day have the power to judge the angels. We can hone the ability, latent within us, to discern the light from the darkness, the good from the evil, the fallen from the unfallen. We have the gift to judge the angels as well as to judge the powers of this world. All we need to do is claim this God-given gift, through prayer and by truly opening our hearts to God.

All too often, we don't acknowledge or exercise our God-given abilities. But we have the discernment, power, and authority to say yes to the light and no to the darkness. We cannot and should not ever judge the salvation of human beings. That is Christ's job. But we can discern our right thoughts and actions in this life. We can choose the light.

In order to judge angels, we must first identify the ways in which they influence us. We must learn to tell the difference between temptation and innovation within the landscape of our own minds. This kind of discernment is highly individualized. Years of counseling and praying with people about their inner struggles have led me to believe that each one of us has a unique spiritual battle, a unique set of tempations. My demons and my angels will look wholly different from yours. Darkness takes on specific forms depending on our life circumstances and our biological makeup as well as the culture in which we were raised. We must be able to name and know our temptations. Jesus does this very thing when he goes out into the desert immediately after his baptism: he learns the types of temptations and importantly, what the tempter sounds like to him. And he is able to resist. Our particular pains and vulnerabilities can offer tremendous insight but also be sources of great temptation.

At the same time, we must learn to recognize the light. What does inspiration look like to you? What does insight, innovation, joy, and love sound like? How can you recognize a truly creative thought that comes to you as a gift from above? Are you listening? Are you paying attention? Perhaps great artists and writers exist all around us but some have never found their art because they have never learned to listen to the creative genius that resides inside them.

We have the power to judge angels. To access and exercise that power, we must spend time with God and listen for the voices of the angels.

Thirty-Nine

Paul's Visit to the Third Heaven

It is necessary to boast; nothing is to be gained by it, but I will go on to visions and revelations of the Lord. I know a person in Christ who fourteen years ago was caught up to the third heaven—whether in the body or out of the body I do not know; God knows. And I know that such a person—whether in the body or out of the body I do not know; God knows—was caught up into Paradise and heard things that are not to be told, that no mortal is permitted to repeat…Therefore, to keep me from being too elated, a thorn was given to me in the flesh, a messenger of Satan to torment me, to keep me from being too elated. Three times I appealed to the Lord about this, that it would leave me, but he said to me, "My grace is sufficient for you, for power is made perfect in weakness."

2 Corinthians 12:1-4, 7-9a

Paul's letters assume the existence of a celestial reality. In all of the epistles, he speaks of angels, of powers and dominions and principalities with the kind of familiarity that can only come from one who has experienced them. He speaks of these beings with a casual certainty, as if he no longer needs to prove their existence. Is his familiarity born of some kind of vision of a heavenly realm, or is it simply the product of the ancient worldview in which he is immersed, a worldview that assumes the existence of spiritual realms?

Paul finds it impossible or somehow forbidden to narrate his own visions of heaven. Is he trying to be humble? Is this some kind of rhetorical device? For reasons unknown, Paul is determined to awkwardly pose his experience in the third person. He says that a man was "caught up" or "snatched up" into heaven. From his description, it sounds as if this vision came rapidly, and it is so real that Paul cannot discern if he is in or out of his body. This experience changes Paul and makes him aware of a reality that many of us can only imagine. Paul is there, "caught up into Paradise." And after his visit, he is never the same. He is wounded somehow, but he also has a source of immense perspective and strength. After this moment, nothing in this life can shake Paul's overwhelming faith in Christ. Prison, beatings, and disagreements in the church: They all seem inconsequential in light of this experience. Paul has seen heaven.

Paul frustrates us by referring to a third heaven but doesn't tell us about the first two. How many heavens are there? What are the angels like? Paul does not say. He doesn't give us details of this third heaven either. He says that in this place he hears things that are not to be repeated. Why is this so? Again, Paul does not explain. He just wants us to know it is there. Perhaps this third heaven defies all explanation. All that seems important to Paul is the fact that he was there. But the experience fills Paul with such joy that God directs a messenger of Satan[13] to afflict him with a thorn in the flesh to bring Paul back to the reality of this broken world. It is almost as if he couldn't stay here on this earth without some kind of suffering to hold him here.

I believe this experience of "third heaven" informs all of Paul's ministry and writings. Though he never again refers directly to this third heaven, it seems to shape his every thought and expression. Paul refers to levels and kinds of angels that are not found anywhere else in scripture. How does he know of these beings, whose existence he seems to assume is real? He must have seen them. There is no other explanation that makes any sense at all.

Forty

WOUNDED BY SATAN

Therefore to keep me from being too elated, a thorn was given to me in the flesh, a messenger of Satan to torment me, to keep me from being too elated. Three times I appealed to the Lord about this, that it would leave me, but he said to me, "My grace is sufficient for you, for power is made perfect in weakness."

2 Corinthians 12:7-8

Mary Neal died in a kayaking accident in South America and after half an hour, she was resuscitated. In her book *To Heaven and Back*, she describes what happened to her after she died, how she saw angels and witnessed a beauty that she has trouble describing in words. One of the remarkable aspects about her account is her desire to stay in heaven. Mary was married and had small children at the time, but she does not hesitate to admit that she wanted to remain in heaven. The beauty and the joy were beyond fathoming. She did not want to return.

Paul also feels such joy when he is snatched up to the "third heaven" that he does not want to return. And so he is given a thorn in the flesh, a wound that changes him, causing him pain and weakness and somehow tethering him to this world. Paul asks the Lord to take away the wound, but God refuses, explaining, "My grace…is made perfect in weakness." Perhaps this thorn in the flesh enhances Paul's message somehow, though in what way, we may never know. Paul never describes this wound. Perhaps it is so obvious that he assumes the people of his churches know of it or will remember from his prior visits. Once again, we have only what we need to know, which is that Paul's visit to heaven ultimately causes him pain here on earth.

Mary Neal too had to return to a broken body and months of rehabilitation. But the journey to physical wellness provided her with the time to digest and to pray about her role in this life. Why did God ask her to return? What was she called to do now? Her physical healing helped her spiritual discernment process, a process that would take over a decade to unfold.

An angel in the very first book of the Bible wounds Jacob. Why would a celestial being wound a person? Why does Paul's wound make him somehow more equipped to return to this life? Why does an angel wound Jacob? It seems that pain and suffering are sometimes vehicles for the advancement of our spiritual lives, ways for us to learn and grow. God uses these wounds to help both Jacob and Paul become all that they are called to be.

Why is grace made perfect in weakness? Why are the poor blessed? How is it possible that the Maker of the Universe would choose pain as a way to manifest glory? Will we ever understand this mystery? Does Paul understand it? I don't think he does, not fully, but he accepts the fact that God will use his pain and weakness to glorify the reality of the divine presence.

Forty-One

THE CELESTIAL HIERARCHY

God put his power to work in Christ when he raised him from the dead and seated him at his right hand in the heavenly places, far above all rule and authority and power and dominion, and above every name that is named, not only in this age but in the age to come.

Ephesians 1:20-21

For in him all things in heaven and on earth were created, things visible and invisible, whether thrones or dominions or rulers or powers—all things have been created through him and for him.

Colossians 1:16

Paul refers to levels of celestial life, beings that exist outside the realm of our physical reality. Paul mentions them only in passing, as levels that Christ rises above during the event of the resurrection. It is as if we are being introduced to a whole other world, but, if it were a tour of a new skyscraper, Paul does not stop to introduce each floor. He takes us instead in an elevator and mentions the floors in passing as we speed by on our way to the throne room where Christ dwells. Paul gives us very little information on each level's design or qualities or even their rank levels. We are left to discern that on our own. What seems important to Paul is the recognition that the spiritual world is a lot more complex than meets the eye, but Christ rises above it all.

As I mentioned in earlier meditations, in an effort to create some kind of order out of Paul's references, the fourth-century theologian Dionysius the Areopagite created a system with nine levels of celestial beings. This angelic hierarchy was Dionysius's attempt to clarify and categorize mysterious phenomena that defy categorization. Despite the obvious inadequacies of his theory, Dionysius's celestial hierarchy was popular in the ancient world for it gave scholars and theologians a way to approach a topic that by its nature was intellectually hard to access. Human beings are far more comfortable with categorizing our own knowledge, even if the categories are invented solely for the purpose of our own familiarity and not from objective research or data. How can we categorize heaven? Though the task is impossible, it is our way to try to understand things that by their very nature transcend our rational minds.

Paul does not seem to think that celestial categories are important. Paul wants us to know that God made all of us: not just the physical world that we see in front of us but also the levels of heaven and the angels in all their forms. In addition, Paul wants us to know that Christ is placed above it all, far above every kind of angel and heavenly being.

Perhaps Paul understands that our attempts to create intellectual order out of the heavenly realms are a futile exercise. He seems comfortable simply reporting their existence on his way up to the throne of God, where Christ sits with the Almighty in glory.

When I was twelve, I discovered there were many levels of depth to the oceans of our world. I felt that I had uncovered a gold mine. There was so much more down there than I had ever imagined—a world of wonder far beyond my fathoming. This discovery led to my increased sense of awe and wonder. There are worlds down there! And there are worlds in heaven too. Paul feels it is enough just for us to know this. As we learn more and more about the universe, we know there are many dimensions or levels of existence. Most are beyond description or intellectual fathoming. We are realizing that Paul's visions may indeed be possible realities.

Fig. 26

Seraphim, cherubim, ancients, thrones, dominions, archangels, angels—
the Bible makes passing reference to many seemingly different kinds of
angelic beings. There is a structure or divine architecture hinted at but
not explained in scripture, an organization of the Earth, the heavens,
and the universe that is the formal expression of God's logic of creation.
In fact, God, the creator of all things, was often thought of as the divine
architect and was depicted in medieval art with an architect's compass,
drawing the blueprint of the spheres of heaven and earth, as in a
medieval copy of the vernacular Bible historiale (Fig. 26).

Artists give form to this logic in many works of medieval and
Renaissance religious art. Visions of heaven depict God the Father or the
Trinity ringed by circles of red seraphs, blue cherubs, and pale angels,
as in a fifteenth-century painting of the celestial hierarchy in a medieval
encyclopedia, the *Miroir historiale*, or *Mirror of History* (Fig. 27). Medieval
thinkers conceived of the universe as a series of concentric circles with
Earth at its center followed by the other three elements—water, air, and
fire—the sun and the moon and the known planets, each in its perfect
orbit, and the stars beyond, as in an image from a fourteenth-century

Fig. 27

copy of the encyclopedic text, the *Breviari d'Amor* (Fig. 28). Medieval scientists extended this vision of the hierarchy of the substances of the physical and visible universe to the metaphysical and invisible cosmos. The orders of angels too were arranged into a celestial hierarchy, and theologians theorized the different spheres of the hells and heavens, as envisioned in the whirling circles of angelic beings in Adriaen Collaert's engraving known by the title, God's Answer to Job (Refer to Fig. 13, page 68).

Of course, humans have known for centuries that Earth and the cosmos exhibit signs of order that can be studied and explained through logic and science: The day yields to night, the cycle of the seasons revolves in tandem with the movements and phases of the sun and the moon, and the planets and stars wheel across the night sky on their eternal paths. Early humans, long before the coming of Christ, recognized that the universe seems to be governed by an orderly power, even if life at the human scale often seems chaotic and unpredictable.

Medieval and Renaissance thinkers blended their interests in religion and science. They found that scientific insight into nature offered confirmation and insight into the chief characteristic of God's creation: its rationality. Medieval scholars understood the universe to be the reflection of the divine intelligence of God as the *Logos*, the Word. According to the Gospel of John, "In the beginning was the Word, and the Word was with God, and the Word was God…All things were made by him." In Genesis, God says a word, "Light," and there was light. This power of God's language and expression to create things, to give them meaning and character and substance, each according to its own kind (Genesis 1) was understood by scientific and religious thinkers as the underlying and true principle of creation: that God's intelligence is rational, that creation is logically ordered, and that it is thus rationally intelligible to us.

In a twelfth-century German missal or Mass book (Fig. 29), the creation is depicted almost like a flowchart. At the top center of the image, God appears higher than all other things, flanked on either side by seraphs. God places hands on top of a large circle or wheel divided by spokes into six radial sections. Each section contains another circular frame,

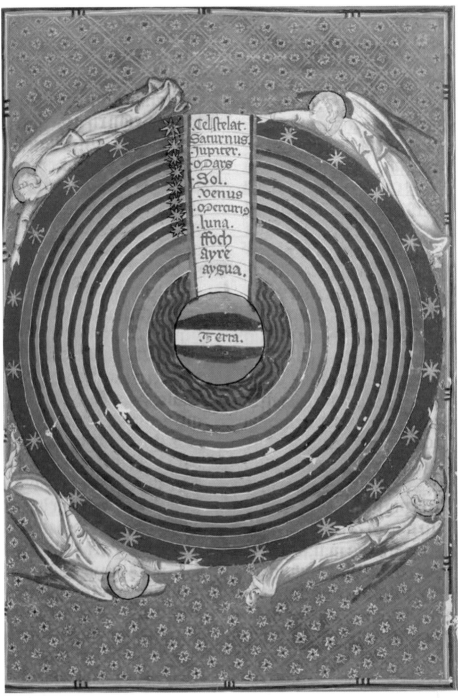

Fig. 28

Fig. 29

with a seventh larger circle at the center of the image. Each of these smaller circles frames one of God's creations: the firmament amidst the waters, the division of light and dark, earth and trees and growing things, birds, beasts, and at the center, human beings. In this diagram of creation, the frame containing the beasts of the earth is linked to the frame around Adam and Eve, connecting human beings and beasts as creatures of God that walk on the earth. The beasts are literally subordinate to human beings in this image, an order below humankind, housed in a smaller frame dependent on the larger circle containing Adam and Eve. This is the artist's way of diagramming two profound ideas: first, the proto-modern idea of orders of classification and second, the moral idea of dominion, of the responsibility and duty of humans, God's creatures, to other creations.

Just as God made things by separating them, defining them, and ordering them, so the root of our science has for centuries been based on distinguishing things, categorizing them, and interpreting them in relation to each other, each according to its kind. We have given names to categories of creatures (orders, families, genuses, and species), to types of tiny particles (protons, electrons, neutrons, quarks, neutrinos, etc.), and to massive celestial objects (quasars, pulsars, nebulae, etc.). Human intelligence has an ordering impulse; we are classifying animals. This makes sense, as we are made in God's image, and the divine intelligence has an ordering imperative.

Fig. 30

In a medieval copy of the works of Boethius (Fig. 30), an early Christian philosopher, a painting of the personification of Philosophy gestures toward heaven, instructing the philosopher on God's role in the universe. God is surrounded by circles of light, by red seraphs and blue cherubs. Philosophy tells Boethius that God has foreknowledge of all things that will be: Having set the universe in motion according to the rational principles that he conceived, God knows all of its movements in advance. This is a spiritual but also a scientific insight into the structure of the universe: As surely as the student of physics—given the variables of mass, velocity, drag, etc.—can calculate the path of the flight of a ball, God knows the past and future positions of all matters.

The glimpses we obtain through scripture of orders of angels, ancients, cherubim, seraphim, and other heavenly beings are like the glimpses of the physical universe offered by mathematics and science. We are able to see and to understand a tiny, particular aspect of a vast and complex system. We are able to know one little thing but also to perceive through it the existence of a larger order that governs the universe at a scale— at once infinitesimally small and infinitely huge—that surpasses our human faculties of perception but that shapes the meaning and purpose of our spiritual, intellectual, and moral lives in God's creation.

Forty-Two

THE EARTHLY STRUGGLE

Put on the whole armor of God, so that you may be able to stand against the wiles of the devil. For our struggle is not against enemies of blood and flesh, but against the rulers, against the authorities, against the cosmic powers of this present darkness, against the spiritual forces of evil in the heavenly places.

Ephesians 6:11-12

I believe our world reflects a cosmic battle between the light and the darkness. Throughout my adult life, the Episcopal Church has been torn apart by a battle over gender and sex, and we have tried valiantly to manage the fight, to be both prophetic and pastoral, but we have neglected to identify with whom we are fighting. We have neglected to realize that it is Satan who happily throws sex into the middle of the church and laughs as we claw ourselves apart about it. Instead of reflecting on matters with thoughtfulness and prayers, we have ploughed ahead, often maligning those who disagree with us, forgetting that they are not the real enemy. We have neglected to fully understand the influence of culture and environment and failed to form personal relationships with the love and respect that it takes to move hearts and change minds. The real enemy is not those with whom we disagree: it is the one who masterfully creates an environment in our country where we view complex and evolving issues with a black-and-white certainty that leaves little room for compassion, disagreement, or compromise. When viewed from this celestial perspective, the devil is having a celebration watching as tens of thousands of people sever relationships, start new denominations, and fight over church buildings. If only we had handled things differently, perhaps we might have found a way to be true to our values while not severing our communities.

Many of the struggles of this life must be viewed from the perspective of a cosmic battle. This perspective is not to take away our responsibility but to put the power where it truly is—in the hands of God. Darkness has power only when the light is not shined upon it. Devils and demons want us unaware of and oblivious to their existence. They want alcoholics to drink themselves to death without knowing they are fighting possession of a demon called addiction. They want anorexics to starve themselves to death, unable to recognize that toxic thinking is destroying their bodies. The devil wants us all to believe we are unloved and unworthy, that we must do something to earn God's love. But we are all children of God and as such, we are good.

Once we can understand and accept that we are beloved children of God often enslaved by demons of addiction, depression, greed, and countless others, then we can take the first step to being truly free and to loving ourselves. No wonder the devil wants to remain in the shadows. Half of the battle is won when we identify who the enemy really is.

Once we know whom we are fighting, then we can put on the armor of God that Saint Paul describes. We clothe ourselves with prayer and lean on scripture and friendship and love that surround us. We realize we are part of a cosmic battle that has been raging since the beginning of the creation. And we discover that we are not alone—and most importantly, that through Christ's triumph over death, the war has already been won.

My sister-in-law runs a rehabilitation program for girls who have been imprisoned. Many of these girls have prostituted themselves for money or drugs—and often, to feel loved. She introduces them to the light of Christ and talks about the darkness of the demons. She emphasizes that they are not alone. The struggle may not end (though it hopefully gets better), but the women come to recognize the cosmic powers of darkness that they have been fighting. Their healing, and ours, begins with the awareness of the enemy.

Forty-Three

Who Really Gets It Done

The Revelation of Jesus Christ, which God gave him to show his servants what must soon take place; he made it known by sending his angel to his servant John, who testified to the word of God and to the testimony of Jesus Christ, even to all that he saw.

Revelation 1:1-2

John of Patmos sees visions of heaven and hears the voice of the Son of God. Like dreams, visions and prophecies are a particular kind of communication from God: They tell us who we are and who God wants us to be. They are not the same as historical fact, and they are not literal future predictions, although John says that these things are to come. John's Revelation from God paints a picture of the end of all days and the coming of the Son of God. In John's vision, angels are everywhere.

It is an angel who initiates the revealing of God's message. And, as we shall see in these next few meditations, angels take on a variety of roles: singing and playing trumpets, yes, but also carrying out violent acts and ushering in the end of the world as we know it. They tear up the planet, battle the devil, and bring the saved into God's presence. They announce the coming of the savior and the end of evil. The angels move efficiently between heaven and earth; They are the initiators, the bridge builders, and the ones who clear the stage at the end of all time. They are the chorus of heavenly song and the executors of God's vision. They are travel companions and guides. And at the end of time, angels play a new role—that of warriors.

It is clear from John's vision that it is the angels who defeat the devil on behalf of God, not us. We humans are marked as belonging to Christ and then we are saved. Like small children, we are saved and dressed as new and brought into the presence of God. The angels clean up the mess that is earth at the end of its days. Angels separate the good from the evil and usher in the age of eternal life. They do the hard work for us, for we are incapable of doing it ourselves.

John of Patmos lives in a time in which Rome is persecuting Christians. The temple in Jerusalem has been destroyed. John has been exiled. Everything seems hopeless. John's vision is God's way of assuring John and the seven churches that he loves that it is not their job to fix everything. *I will do that*, God says. *I am in control and, though everything seems hopeless, I will defeat evil and I will usher in the end of time and the beginning of a new life that will last forever.*

And whom will God use to get this done? Not us, for we need a savior. No, God will enlist the help of the angels.

Forty-Four

Seven Angels for Seven Churches

Now write what you have seen, what is, and what is to take place after this. As for the mystery of the seven stars that you saw in my right hand, and the seven golden lampstands: the seven stars are the angels of the seven churches, and the seven lampstands are the seven churches. "To the angel of the church in Ephesus write…"

Revelation 1:19—2:1

John writes to seven churches, all of whom he knows and loves. Similar to Paul who writes letters to churches, John wants to share specific instructions to each unique church, instructions that he believes come from God. But John addresses his letters not directly to the churches themselves but to the angel who protects each church. John assumes each worshiping community has a specific angelic presence that watches over it and is assigned to bring messages to that church from God. This is the closest thing we find to a guardian angel in the New Testament.

I have been a priest for twenty years. I have served in four churches during that time, and each church has been unique. There is a personality that each community develops, a sense of self that is much more than a mission statement or a strategic plan. A church community has an essence, a way of being, a unique vocation that leads them to manifest the love of God into the world. Each community has a certain flavor, a certain purpose, and God calls each to a particular role in its neighborhood and in the world. To be sure, specific factors influence this call, including the gifts of the members of the church, available resources, and the facilities, but nevertheless a unique spirit lives within each church community. Perhaps part of this unique spirit comes from an assigned angel, a messenger from God to those who are praying and asking for guidance, a source of strength and a protector against all those forces of wickedness that would tear a church apart.

Seven angels for the seven churches, each bringing a special message of hope, correction, and encouragement. Many churches are named after a patron saint, and often that saint shapes our identity as a community. I wonder if it might be wise for us to gather our church communities and ask ourselves: Do we have an angel to guide us in discerning God's will? And if so, what kind of message is that angel bringing to us?

Forty-Five

SANCTUS

And the four living creatures, each of them with six wings, are full of eyes all around and inside. Day and night without ceasing they sing, "Holy, holy, holy, the Lord God the Almighty, who was and is and is to come."

Revelation 4:8

Christian denominations worship differently. Roman Catholics, Eastern Orthodox, Lutherans, and Episcopalians worship using an ancient liturgical practice called the eucharist. The word in Greek means thanksgiving. We gather together, and the priest stands behind an altar and retells the story of Jesus' last night with us, how he broke bread and drank wine and shared them with us, instructing us that, when we did this, we were to remember him. These more ancient traditions believe that Christ himself is mystically present in the bread and the wine, though the denominations often disagree on how exactly this is so. By the middle of the second century, many Christians had adopted this poetry as part of the language of their worship services.

Inherent in these traditions is the understanding that God is potently present at the moment when the bread and wine are consecrated. In fact, Eastern Orthodox theologians describe a mystical moment that transcends time itself. In other words, time is changed, and we are present with Christ and with the angels around the altar in heaven itself. Angels and archangels and all the company of heaven surround us. They are with us right here, right now, and we cannot see them.

What does this mean? It means that these early Christians conceived of the presence of heavenly beings in our lives here on earth. In the Greek of the New Testament, there are two words for time: *chronos* and *kairos*. We humans perceive our existence in chronological time, time that moves only forward. But God lives in *kairos* time, transcending our linear idea of time so that God is present both at the Last Supper with Jesus and at our altar in Brooklyn, New York, on a Sunday. God can be present at the altar of a church without walls where homeless gather and at the high altar of a cathedral in Paris and in heaven itself all at the same time. And with God, the angels are present too.

This leads us to return to the concept of time as revealed in quantum mechanics. If time is the fourth dimension, then God and the angels exist in dimensions far beyond that. God is, quite simply, able to be everywhere at once. And with God are the angels.

Imagine the distinct possibility that angels are flying right in front of you right now. Imagine God is communicating with you all the time and in myriad ways. Prayer is not about you initiating contact with God: God has been reaching out to you from the very moment when you were conceived and knit together in your mother's womb. A song of love is being sung to you all your life, and it will never end. You are invited to join in the song.

Forty-Six

ANGELS SING AND ANGELS WORSHIP

Then I looked, and I heard the voice of many angels surrounding the throne and the living creatures and the elders; they numbered myriads of myriads and thousands of thousands, singing with full voice, "Worthy is the Lamb that was slaughtered to receive power and wealth and wisdom and might and honor and glory and blessing!"

Revelation 5:11-12

And all the angels stood around the throne and around the elders and the four living creatures, and they fell on their faces before the throne and worshiped God, singing, "Amen! Blessing and glory and wisdom and thanksgiving and honor and power and might be to our God forever and ever! Amen."

Revelation 7:11-12

John of Patmos's vision is chock full of angels. Angels surround the throne of God, perpetually singing in an act of eternal worship. These angels never stop their worship. They never stop their singing. This is not a broken-record kind of redundancy; it is the repetition of eternal beings that have found exactly what they are meant to do. It is akin to water flowing in a river: It just goes and goes and goes. It never ends. It is a constant flow of love and adoration to God.

I believe the purpose of human love is to learn to love God and by extension to love our neighbor. One of the best ways to express the love of God is through worship, with the kind of praise and adoration that opens the heart and transports a person into the divine presence. This is why we were made: to sing praises to our Maker. Music defies human understanding. It touches and moves us in ways that we cannot otherwise access. No wonder angels sing. I have always believed music is the language of heaven.

When parents bring a child to me for baptism, I try to explain how essential worship is to the developing human being. I ask them what they want their child to grow up to be like. They answer very similarly: a good person, someone who seeks justice, someone who tells the truth, someone who is content. I explain that they cannot protect their child from all pain in this world, but they can make the child's relationship with God central to the child's life. One way to model that is to place worship as the highest priority. Nothing is more important than worship. Nothing will shape the heart of a human like the love of God in practice: not violin or soccer or even school. There is simply nothing more important than worship for it expresses our core nature and teaches us to worship God instead of ourselves.

What do angels do in heaven? They worship. That's all they do, and they never stop.

THE ARCHANGEL MICHAEL AND THE DRAGON

Michael the Archangel is one of the most famed and recognizable of God's angels, the subject of thousands of paintings, sculptures, prints, medals, and other works. Michael is beloved and remembered as the foremost of the guardian angels, a valiant protector, wearing the armor of God, wielding the sword of faith in conquest of the devil, as in a fifteenth-century altarpiece from Spain (Fig. 31).

The most indelible image of Michael in scripture comes from the Book of Revelation, from John's vision of a war in heaven between Michael, his angelic army, and the dragon who is Satan and his rebel angels (Revelation 12:7-13). In John's vision, Michael defeats the dragon, who is cast down to earth, where he makes war on the followers of Christ. This vision is one that poses many questions and challenges to our understanding. Perhaps most important, though the devil is cast out of heaven, why does God allow Satan to wreak havoc and to persecute the earth?

In a famous woodcut by the German artist Albrecht Dürer (Fig. 32), this dilemma is expressed visually. Michael in the center, surrounded by his angels, does battle with the dragon and his fellow rebels. The angels are stern but beautiful human warriors, while the rebel angels are the stuff of nightmares: bat-winged, snake-tailed, scaly, spiky, skeletal, and rotten-looking creatures. The war in heaven occupies the top three-quarters on the composition. It is busy with lines and heavy with ink, while the bottom quarter of the picture is reserved for the depiction of the earth, which is by contrast light, open, peaceful, and inviting. The implication of the picture is clear. Though earth seems peaceful now, a landscape of orderly towns, church steeples, and ships at sea, soon all hell will break loose.

Fig. 31

Fig. 32

Medieval theologians generally interpret this passage of Revelation, from the very end of the Bible, in relation to Genesis and the very beginning. The dragon, the devil, is that same serpent who tempted Adam and Eve in the Garden, who was punished along with our human ancestors. God cursed the serpent, "Upon your belly you shall go, and dust you shall eat all the days of your life. I will put enmity between you and the woman, and between your offspring and hers; he will strike your head, and you will strike his heel" (Genesis 3:14-15). This curse echoes in John's vision, in which the dragon cast from heaven into the earth pursues the woman "clothed with the sun" and "went off to make war on the rest of her children." The serpent lies in wait for our heel, as God warned. For better or worse, sinners and their tempter—human beings and the devil—are cast out of paradise together and must contend with each other until the end of time.

The vision of Michael, however, in victory over the dragon, is a vision of hope and salvation. The devil can be defeated. Indeed, the lesson is that he only has power in the earth. The fourth-century theologian Tyconius, for example, citing the example of Job, observes that Satan received authority from God only to fight with the children of the woman. In Tyconius's view, this makes the followers of Christ part of Michael's army. He writes that John "calls Christ 'Michael' and holy people 'his angels.'"

A superb illuminated initial in a thirteenth-century medieval prayer book (Fig. 33) depicts Michael standing atop the dragon, piercing the beast with a long spear or lance. Michael is surrounded by twining tendrils of vine-scroll interlace inhabited by grotesques and monstrous heads that evoke the rebel angels. Below left, outside the edge of the letter "Q," a person in red kneels, supporting the letter like an Atlas-figure, bearing its weight on his shoulders. This little figure symbolizes the earth and us, and his physical struggle and effort is the sign of our spiritual struggle. The painted letter is the initial of the psalmic prayer, *Quid glorias in malicia,* "Why dost thou glory in malice, thou that art mighty in iniquity?" (Psalm 51:3 in the Latin Vulgate). This is a psalm of David that refers to one of the most terrible events in Israel during David's life. When David was pursued by Saul, he took refuge with the priest Ahimelech, a righteous man and descendant of Aaron. Doeg the

Fig. 33

Edomite, one of Saul's servants, informed the king that Ahimelech
had aided David. Saul ordered the deaths of the Ahimelech and his
brethren, and Doeg slew eighty-five priests at the king's command (1
Samuel 22). It is hard to imagine a greater injustice or more awful
sacrilege than the murder of these holy men.

For medieval interpreters, this story contains a prophecy of Christ and of the war in heaven. Saul signifies death and the devil, the wicked Doeg is understood to prefigure Antichrist, the house of Ahimelech symbolizes heaven, while Ahimelech and David both are interpreted as aspects of Christ himself. Ahimelech, who dies, is the priestly and sacrificial aspect of Christ, who dies on the cross on earth pursued by the devil. David is the image of Christ the King, who will triumph over death and the devil. In this and other prayer books in which the image of Michael adorns the words of Psalm 51, Michael's victory over the dragon is not meant to be understood as the sign that victory has been won but that the war is being fought, that we also are part of it, on one side or the other. The picture and the prayer offer images of our struggle meant to rally the better angels of our natures.

For medieval and Renaissance interpreters, the idea of a war in heaven signifies a war in the Church, the idea that it is in the active practice and the living or our faith that the battle is lost or won. The Church is a place of comfort and help, yes, just as Ahimelech provided help to David, but medieval theologians see the war in heaven as a reminder not to take the Church for granted but to understand that this is where we must actively fight the good fight. This is the meaning of images of Michael and the Dragon that often adorned the crozier or staff carried by bishops in the medieval church. A thirteenth-century French crozier head (Fig. 34) curves around in imitation of the ancient shepherd's crook, forming a "Q" at the top, perhaps in reference to the Quid glorias in malicia prayer. Michael with his spear attacks the dragon, whose tail forms the tail of the "Q," while the circle of the "Q" transforms at the end into a serpent's head that is attacking Michael from behind. In this image, the battle is not won. The struggle is ongoing. The image of Michael transforms the bishop's staff into a weapon, a spear like that wielded by the archangel, and the bishop is revealed to be a warrior of heaven, like Ahimelech and his priests, defending against the devil. Life and soul hang in the balance of this eternal conflict.

Fig. 34

Forty-Seven

ANGELS BRING DESTRUCTION

Then I heard a loud voice from the temple telling the seven angels, "Go and pour out on the earth the seven bowls of the wrath of God."

Revelation 16:1

One of the most brutal parts of the book of Revelation is the plagues. People on earth are flooded with sores, water is turned into blood, the earth is visited with locusts, and more. And guess who pours out this tribulation? Angels. The seven angels disburse seven deadly plagues that remind us of the plagues of the story of the Exodus. These painful afflictions are designed to kill but also to call people to repentance. As in Exodus, the plagues are signs of great and tumultuous change and ultimately, of hope for a future without oppression.

For the modern reader, the plagues of Revelation seem cruel and unacceptable. What kind of God sends angels to make people miserable? Why does John of Patmos have this vision? Remember that John lives in a time of great oppression and great hopelessness. From his perspective, the only way to cleanse the earth of evil and to teach repentance is for God to shake things up. For John, it is like the deep cleaning of a filthy house. A lot needs to be thrown away; much needs to be stripped down and burned off and cleansed. And who else can do such massive work but angels?

Why does it take pain to liberate us from situations that are unacceptable? Right now public school teachers across the country are staging massive strikes. They have halted all their teaching to fight for higher wages. They believe this difficult action of inflicting pain is the only way to motivate the comfortable into action. Children are going without education. Parents are struggling to find childcare. Yet the teachers understand that those in authority, those who are comfortable and are making higher wages, are not likely to change unless they are made so drastically uncomfortable that their situation cannot continue. Pain is a motivator.

So too with our bodies. It can be difficult to grow old, with new aches and pains surfacing each day, and yet, if a person is listening to God and to love, this process also yields wisdom and gratitude and a kind of readiness for the life hereafter. No one appreciates health like one who has been sick. If we never experience physical pain, we might never learn to care for our bodies or to appreciate their miraculous ability to heal. Pain is a teacher.

I hate to think of angels spreading destruction, but John offers a vision of just that, of angels who are good and who come from God pouring down violence in the hope that those who want to be with God will turn and be saved. Will we ever understand why people suffer? Not in this life, but we can listen to the pain and learn from it. We can learn to be dependent on God alone. That is something that we can understand.

Forty-Eight

HELL

Then I saw an angel coming down from heaven, holding in his hand the key to the bottomless pit and a great chain. He seized the dragon, that ancient serpent, who is the Devil and Satan, and bound him for a thousand years, and threw him into the pit, and locked and sealed it over him, so that he would deceive the nations no more.

Revelation 20:1-3a

Satan is a fallen angel. He is defeated by Archangel Michael and sent to hell for all eternity. The Book of Revelation tells us that both fallen angels and some human beings will end up in eternal torment. Jesus himself mentions a place where there is weeping and gnashing of teeth; he says it is possible for God to throw people into hell.

For many modern minds, the idea of hell is morally repugnant. What kind of loving God allows creatures that are divinely made to live in torment and suffering? Doesn't God want us all happy and well and successful and well-balanced? If God is love, why does God allow us to suffer that much, no matter how awful our deeds?

Author C.S. Lewis handled this problem masterfully by envisioning hell with an open door. He proposed that it is always possible to leave hell and enter heaven if one has the will to do the painful work of repentance.[14] But the Book of Revelation makes this fiery pit sound like it lasts forever. And when Jesus tells a parable about Lazarus and the rich man, the rich man tries to come to heaven but Abraham the great prophet explains that one cannot cross the border between heaven and hell. So which is true? Is it possible to repent and make your way out of hell or is the decision of our salvation made once and for all eternity?[15] I am not sure that we humans will ever master the complex mystery of our salvation. For our purposes, I think it is sufficient to know that our actions matter. Our prayers matter. We live this life as preparation for something more, and this life affects what happens after we die. Beyond that, the rest is up to God.

We are not alone in this. Revelation shares that the angels are separated, and their salvation determined at the end of days. Some angels will end up in hell and others in heaven. This makes sense because we receive messages or influences that are holy and good and true, and we are also influenced by temptation and hatred and revenge. The messengers of God clearly come in two very different forms: Some to guide us to God and others to bring misery and total self-absorption. The battle between heaven and hell goes on all the time inside each of us.

Forty-Nine

The Great Battle

When the thousand years are ended, Satan will be released from his prison and will come out to deceive the nations at the four corners of the earth, Gog and Magog, in order to gather them for battle; they are as numerous as the sands of the sea. They marched up over the breadth of the earth and surrounded the camp of the saints and the beloved city. And fire came down from heaven and consumed them. And the devil who had deceived them was thrown into the lake of fire and sulfur, where the beast and the false prophet were, and they will be tormented day and night forever and ever.

Revelation 20:7-10

We all love the great action movies. *Star Wars* is one of my favorites. I love to see the battle between good and evil. I want to stand up and cheer when good triumphs! It is as if something primal, something of my essence, is being expressed on the screen. I love that the battle lines are clear: when the bad characters come on, they look ugly and mean and scary music plays. When the heroes appear, the music changes to some bold, strong tempo, and they are usually good looking and just, well, good. The battle is so straightforward, so clear. And it is the clarity that I find most gratifying.

The rest of my life is not so clear. I find elements of both good and evil within my own mind, much less within my loved ones and friends. A close friend will be sweet one day and then bite my head off the next day for no apparent reason. A church prayer group will become divided and enslaved by gossip. We chalk these things up to stress or selfishness or a rough day, but the truth is that we all have both good and evil within our very selves. The battle is raging inside of us and that is why it is such a relief to escape to the movies, where the lines are clearly drawn.

John's vision includes a great battle between the archangel Michael and the Great Dragon. In his vision, like in a good action flick, it is very clear who is good and who is evil. Michael comes from the throne of God, and the Dragon appears like a larger and more vivid form of the snake in the Garden of Eden.

Sometimes when I feel desperate, I pray to Archangel Michael, the great warrior, for rescue. After all, in John's vision, Michael not only throws down the Dragon, but he also locks him up forever. FOREVER. There is no more confusion, no more blurry lines, no more distraction or temptation or fear. The Dragon is gone, and we are free to love God as we were originally created to do. It is the ultimate happy ending.

The Book of Revelation is violent and scary but also incredibly gratifying. The enemy finally faces his equal in an angel. We have been given a warrior to fight on our behalf. He is our champion, our rescuer, our pride and joy. He does what we cannot, and all is made clear for us. All of this is God's doing and God's victory. God is the rescuer and redeemer who sends the angels to win the victory. We can watch the battle and cheer. And when it is over, we can live forever.

Fifty

JOINING IN

Then an angel showed me the river of the water of life,
bright as crystal, flowing from the throne of God and of the
Lamb through the middle of the street of the city. On either
side of the river is the tree of life with its twelve kinds of
fruit, producing its fruit each month; and the leaves of the
tree are for the healing of the nations.

Revelation 22:1-2

Just as an angel stood at the gate of Eden to bar us from entering once we had fallen from God's grace, so an angel leads us back to the new Jerusalem. Eden has now been replaced by a paradise more glorious than before. And in the midst of paradise is the tree of life, just as it was in the beginning. But this time, we are invited to eat.

Our relationship with angels is reflective of our relationship with Jesus. When we are estranged from God and Christ, an angel will bar our way to paradise until we are ready to return home. And when we are ready and the angels have defeated all evil and all fear, they will lead us back to the place where we were once forbidden to go. They will lead us home.

The place of angels in the narrative of scripture cannot be underestimated. They are our guides, our friends, and protectors. They keep the boundaries that are set for us so that we might become all that we are called to be. They are agents of goodness and light, bodily manifestations of God's love and wisdom. They are vital to our understanding of salvation and eternal life.

How is it that we have relegated these beings to Hallmark cards? How is it that we have forgotten their vital role in the narrative of salvation? Just because we cannot see angels does not mean that they aren't there. They are with us all the time; we have simply fallen asleep and forgotten their magnificence.

To entertain the presence of angels is to recognize that salvation is not our doing. No, scripture is clear that we don't fix this broken world: Christ does this with the help of the angels. All we need to do is trust in their power and magnificence and do the work that God is calling us to do. The story is written. God is in charge. We will all awaken to a new world where there is no darkness. The angels of light win. They always win, for God is good. That is the good news.

Afterword

This book is a journey into an area of scripture that has long been overlooked by many modern Christians in mainline denominations. Some of these passages may have been unfamiliar or made you uncomfortable. The rational mind can't comprehend the full mystery of angels. It is an act of bravery to read this book and to contemplate this mystical realm. I don't present this material with any kind of prescription or advice other than to let these passages wash over you, to give yourself the freedom to reflect and respond.

It is my hope that the artwork featured in these pages assists you in your contemplation, for angels must be approached much as we would approach a beautiful piece of art, not to understand its constitution but to stand in awe of its beauty. You need not feel that you have to understand or accept the realm of the angelic world. It is simply there for you to ponder, to wonder, to gaze upon.

I find that the more I contemplate these spiritual realities of angels, the more willing I am to accept my role as a beloved child of God who is precious beyond imagining—and yet also small and limited in my understanding and in my abilities. In other words, to contemplate the realm of the spiritual is ultimately to move beyond my self-centeredness and to realize that the world will not be saved by me but by the One who made me and by the angels who serve that One. It is not up to me or to you. And as much as our media and culture would like us to believe, nothing we buy and no action we perform will solve the world's problems. We are to do the best we can to serve the good, but we must always ask for help from realms above.

Amen.

Illustration Credits

1 Eden

Figure 1 Master of Jean de Mandeville (French), *The Expulsion from Paradise*, about 1360-1370, Tempera colors, gold leaf, gold paint, and ink on parchment, Ms. 1, v1, fol. 10v (Photo: The J. Paul Getty Museum, Los Angeles)

Figure 2 Queen Mary Master, Queen Mary Psalter, *Expulsion from the Garden of Eden*, ca. 1310-1320, England, Royal Ms. 2 B VII, f. 4 (Photo: The British Library)

Figure 3 Giovanni di Paolo (Giovanni di Paolo di Grazia), *The Creation of the World and the Expulsion from Paradise*, 1445, Italian, Tempera and gold on wood (Photo: The Metropolitan Museum of Art, New York)

Figure 4 Daniel Fröschl, *The Expulsion from Paradise*, late 16th–early 17th century, Gouache, on vellum (Photo: The Metropolitan Museum of Art, New York)

2 Abraham

Figure 5 Basilica of San Vitale, *Abraham with the Angels at Mamre and the Sacrifice of Abraham*, 547, Mosaic, Ravenna, Italy

Figure 6 Simon Bening (Flemish), *Abraham Washing the Feet of the Three Angels*, about 1525-1530, Tempera colors, gold paint, and gold leaf on parchment, Ms. Ludwig IX 19, fol. 88 (Photo: The J. Paul Getty Museum, Los Angeles)

Figure 7 Master of James IV of Scotland (Flemish), *Abraham and the Three Angels*, about 1510-1520, Tempera colors, gold, and ink on parchment, Ms. Ludwig IX 18, fol. 11 (Photo: The J. Paul Getty Museum, Los Angeles)

3 Job

Figure 8 Delftware Plate with *Job on the Dunghill*, ca. 1650-1670, earthenware with tin glaze (Photo: Rijksmuseum, Amsterdam)

Figure 9 Georg Pencz, *Job on the Dunghill Visited by his Wife and Friends*, 1544-1548, German, Engraving (Photo: Rijksmuseum, Amsterdam)

Figure 10 Follower of the Egerton Master (French / Netherlandish), *Job Derided by his Wife and Friends*, about 1410, Tempera colors, gold leaf, gold paint, and ink on parchment Ms. Ludwig IX 5, fol. 155 (Photo: The J. Paul Getty Museum, Los Angeles)

Figure 11 Simon Bening (Flemish), *Border with Job Mocked by His Wife and Tormented by Two Devils*, about 1525–1530, Tempera colors, gold paint, and gold leaf on parchment, Ms. Ludwig IX 19, fol. 155 (Photo: The J. Paul Getty Museum, Los Angeles)

Figure 12 Follower of the Egerton Master (French / Netherlandish), *Job Pointing to a Blooming Shrub*, about 1410, Tempera colors, gold leaf, gold paint, and ink on parchment, Ms. Ludwig IX 5, fol. 145v (Photo: The J. Paul Getty Museum, Los Angeles)

Figure 13 Adriaen Collaert after Jan van der Straet, *God's Answer to Job*, 1587-1591, Engraving (Photo: Rijksmuseum, Amsterdam)

4 Isaiah
Figure 14 Anonymous, *The Twenty-Four Elders Pay Homage to the Throne of God*, The Getty Apocalypse, about 1255-1260, Tempera colors, gold leaf, colored washes, pen and ink on parchment, Ms. Ludwig III 1, fol. 4v (Photo: The J. Paul Getty Museum, Los Angeles)

Figure 15 Chasse of Champagnat, *Censing Angels with the Hand of God* above, *Christ between Saint Mary and Saint Martial* below, ca. 1150, French, Copper: engraved and gilt; Champlevé enamel (Photo: The Metropolitan Museum of Art, New York)

Figure 16 Chasse of Champagnat, *The Four Living Creatures*, ca. 1150, French, Copper: engraved and gilt; Champlevé enamel (Photo: The Metropolitan Museum of Art, New York)

Figure 17 Workshop of Master of the First Prayer Book of Maximilian (Flemish), *Christ in Majesty*, about 1510–1520, Tempera colors, gold, and ink on parchment, Ms. Ludwig IX 18, fol. 9 (Photo: The J. Paul Getty Museum, Los Angeles)

Figure 18 Andrea Mantegna, *Madonna and Child with Seraphim and Cherubim*, ca. 1454 Italian, Tempera and gold on wood (Photo: The Metropolitan Museum of Art, New York)

Figure 19 Master of Gerona (Italian), *Initial A: Christ in Majesty with Isaiah*, late 13th century, Tempera colors, gold leaf, and ink on parchment Ms. Ludwig VI 6, fol. 2 (Photo: The J. Paul Getty Museum)

5 Annunciation
Figure 20 Spitz Master (French), *The Annunciation*, about 1420, Tempera colors, gold, and ink on parchment, Ms. 57, fol. 50 (Photo: The J. Paul Getty Museum, Los Angeles)

Figure 21 Paolo Veneziano (Italian, Venetian), *The Annunciation*, about 1348–1350, Tempera and gold leaf on panel (Photo: The J. Paul Getty Museum, Los Angeles)

Figure 22 Hendrick Goltzius after Maerten de Vos, *Annunciation*, ca. 1577-1582, Engraving (Photo: Rijksmuseum, Amsterdam)

Figure 23 Anonymous, *The Annunciation*, South German (Bavarian?), Oil and gold on linden (Photo: The Metropolitan Museum of Art, New York)

Figure 24 Gerard David, *Archangel Gabriel and The Virgin Annunciate*, ca. 1510, Netherlandish, Oil on oak panel (Photo: The Metropolitan Museum of Art, New York)

Figure 25 Workshop of Robert Campin, *Annunciation Triptych (Merode Altarpiece)*, ca. 1427-32, Netherlandish, Oil on oak (Photo: The Metropolitan Museum of Art, New York)

6 Celestial Hierarchy
Figure 26 First Master of the Bible Historiale of Jean de Berry (French), *God as Divine Architect*, about 1390-1400, Tempera colors, colored washes, gold leaf, and ink on parchment, Ms. Ludwig XIII 3, leaf 1 (Photo: The J. Paul Getty Museum, Los Angeles)

Figure 27 Anonymous, *God the Father with the Heavenly Hierarchy*, about 1475, Tempera colors, gold leaf, and gold paint on parchment, Ms. Ludwig XIII 5, v1, fol. 27 (Photo: The J. Paul Getty Museum, Los Angeles)

Figure 28 Atelier of the Catalan Master of St. Mark, *Circular diagram of the spheres of the Ptolemaic system*, in Matfré Ermengau of Béziers's *Breviari d'Amor*, last quarter of the 14th century (Photo: The British Library)

Figure 29 Anonymous, *The Creation of the World*, probably 1170s, Tempera colors, gold leaf, silver leaf, and ink on parchment, Ms. 64, fol. 10v (Photo: The J. Paul Getty Museum, Los Angeles)

Figure 30 Coëtivy Master (Henri de Vulcop?) (French), *Philosophy Instructing Boethius on the Role of God*, about 1460-1470, Tempera colors, gold leaf, and gold paint on parchment, Ms. 42, leaf 3 (Photo: The J. Paul Getty Museum, Los Angeles)

7 Michael
Figure 31 Master of Belmonte, *Saint Michael*, 1450–1500, Spanish, Tempera and oil on wood (Photo: The Metropolitan Museum of Art, New York)

Figure 32 Albrecht Dürer, *Saint Michael Fighting the Dragon*, from The Apocalypse, 1511, German, Woodcut (Photo: The Metropolitan Museum of Art, New York)

Figure 33 *Initial Q: Saint Michael and the Dragon*, about 1240-1250, Tempera colors, gold leaf, and silver leaf on parchment, Ms. Ludwig VIII 2, fol. 61v (Photo: The J. Paul Getty Museum, Los Angeles)

Figure 34 Head of a Crozier with Saint Michael Slaying the Dragon, 1220-30, French, Champlevé enamel, copper-gilt, glass paste (Photo: The Metropolitan Museum of Art, New York)

Endnotes

1   I recommend Strong's *Concordance*.
2   Bernard of Clairvaux, "He Who Dwells," *Sermons on the Psalm*.
3   An angel of the Lord will give a similar message of liberation and covenant to the people in chapter two of Judges. The Israelites weep as they recognize their failure to follow God's command and as they anticipate the hardships that they will have to endure on account of their actions.
4   The psalms feature many references to angels. This is one example of one presentation of angels, but I encourage you to read through the psalms and explore and encounter all kinds of angels.
5   Acts 17:34
6   Angels of destruction can be found in both the Old and New Testaments. See Judges 5:23, II Samuel 24:16-17, II Kings 19:35, I Chronicles 21:15-30.
7   Wink, Walter. *Engaging the Powers: Discernment and Resistance in a World of Domination.* Fortress Press, 1992. p. 10.
8   For more on the devil, demons, and the landscape of the mind, see my book, *Healed: How Mary Magdalene was Made Well.* Church Publishing, 2018.
9   Follet, Chelsea, "Five graphs that will change your mind about poverty." Human Progress. March 1, 2017.
10   O'Donohue, John. *Walking in Wonder: Eternal Wisdom for a Modern Mind.* Convergent Books, 2015. p. 22.
11   Osirus, Khalil. *A Freedom that Comes from Within.* Osirus Publishing, 2018.
12   The Greek word *theatron* is here translated as spectacle, but it really means theater or performance. We disciples have become the performers, and the angels are the audience. They are watching us as one would watch a great show, an artistic performance, or a dance on a stage.
13   Here it should be noted that God directs and angel of Satan to cause Paul to suffer. Is Satan used to keep us humble and grounded? Could this be another function of the angels of darkness?
14   Lewis, C.S. *The Great Divorce.* Geoffrey Bles, 1945.
15   The best book on this subject that I have found is by Jerry L. Walls called *Hell: The Logic of Damnation.* University of Notre Dame Press, 1992.

Acknowledgments

I want to thank my family, my husband, JD, and my three sons, Luke, Jake, and Max, who have always supported me both as a priest and as a writer. I also want to thank St. John's Cathedral, the staff, vestry, and parishioners who have encouraged me to teach and preach some of this material and have worked as a sounding board on so much of it.

Thank you to my prayer group, to the Rev. Susan Sharpe who encourage me to write, and to Scott Brown for his brilliance. I would also like to thank Forward Movement, especially Richelle Thompson and consultant David Creech, for their superb editing and thoughtful comments, and Alexis Caoili for her compelling design.

Most of all, I thank God for the ability to put my thoughts into words and to ponder the mystery of this extraordinary life.

About The Author

Katherine B. (Kate) Moorehead is the tenth dean of St. John's Episcopal Cathedral in Jacksonville, Florida. Kate graduated Phi Beta Kappa from Vassar College and graduated *cum laude* with a master of divinity degree from Virginia Theological Seminary. She is the author of six books, *Between Two Worlds: Daily Readings for Advent; Organic God: Lenten Meditations on the Words of Jesus; I Witness: Living Inside the Stories of Advent and Christmas; Get Over Yourself: God's Here; Resurrecting Easter;* and *Healed: The Truth about Mary Magdalene.* Kate and her husband, James (J.D.), have three sons, Luke, Jake, and Max and two Labrador retrievers.

About The Contributor

Scott Brown is an art historian specializing in medieval and Renaissance religious art and architecture. He received his doctorate in the history of art from Yale University and serves as a professor of art history at the University of North Florida. He has published widely on art, liturgy, and religious ritual in medieval art and on the iconography and artistic representation of biblical women. His recent book, *The Riddle of Jael: The History of a Poxied Heroine in Medieval and Renaissance Art and Culture,* is the first book on the representation of the notorious biblical heroine, Jael (Judges 4:18-22). His current research investigates the revival of religious architecture and sculpture linked to the Gregorian reform movement in the eleventh-century Church. Scott and his wife, Sally Anne, have a daughter, Benedicte Eloise.

About Forward Movement

Forward Movement is committed to inspiring disciples and empowering evangelists. Our ministry is lived out by creating resources such as books, small-group studies, apps, and conferences. Our daily devotional, *Forward Day by Day*, is also available in Spanish (*Adelante Día a Día*) and Braille, online, as a podcast, and as an app for smartphones or tablets. It is mailed to more than fifty countries, and we donate nearly 30,000 copies each quarter to prisons, hospitals, and nursing homes. We actively seek partners across the church and look for ways to provide resources that inspire and challenge. A ministry of the Episcopal Church for over eighty years, Forward Movement is a nonprofit organization funded by sales of resources and by gifts from generous donors.

To learn more about Forward Movement and our resources, visit www.ForwardMovement.org. We are delighted to be doing this work and invite your prayers and support.